The Elven Way:

The Magical Path of the Shining Ones

By The Silver Elves

Copyright © 2013 The Silver Elves, Michael J Love and Martha C. Love

All rights reserved.

ISBN-13: 9781482672466
ISBN-10: 1482672464

Printed in the United States of America by CreateSpace

Without limiting the rights under the copyright reserved above, no part of this publication may be reproduced, stored in or introduced into a retrieval system, or transmitted in any form or by any means (electronic, mechanical, by photocopying, recording or otherwise) without the prior written permission of the copyright owner and the publisher of the book.

DEDICATION

This book is dedicated to The Shining Ones, our beloved kindred, who have guided and protected us our entire lives. We will meet you in Faerie by and by.

> "WE CALL IT THE ELVEN WAY BUT WE COULD CALL IT THE FAERIE WAY, THE FAIR WAY, THE WAY OF THE FAE, THE WAY OF THE SHINING ONES, OR EVEN THE WAY THAT BEGINS IN YOUR DREAMS AND ENDS IN THE LIFE MAGICAL."
> —THE SILVER ELVES

TABLE OF CONTENTS

CHAPTER 1:

AWAKENING 11

The Awakening 12

The Magical Mind 17

The Elven Star 18

Becoming Our Own True S'Elves 19

The Evolution of Power 21

S'elf Sacrifice 24

Higher Mind 25

Elven Sages 26

Evolution: Spiritual and Mundane 27

CHAPTER 2:

STEPPING ONTO THE PATH 31

CHAPTER 3:

ESOTERIC EDUCATION 37

Magical Sacrifice 42

Going One's Way 43

Service 47

CHAPTER 4:

THE SHIELD OF NORMALCY 51

Taking the Gates of Heaven By Storm 52

Raising One's Shield 55

Guardian Angels...56

Bright Dawn of the Soulful Spirit 58

The Dark Mirror 59

CHAPTER 5:

THE SANCTUARY 65

The Harmonies of Elfin 69

Energy, Vibration and Spin 70

Building Form..71

Creation, Stability and Destruction 73

Past Lives 74

Recapitulation..75

The Seven Chakras 76

CHAPTER 6:

THE PROBATIONARY PERIOD 81

Meaning and Purpose 83

Getting Ahead of Ones'elf 85

Vows of Poverty 86

Transpersonality 89

Suffering 91

Poetic Justice 92

The Transference of Power 94

Evoke Often 95

We Are Magic 96

CHAPTER 7:

REALMS AND DIMENSIONS 101

Opting Out 111

The Hierarchy of Evolutionary Elfhood 112

CHAPTER 8:

HARMONIC ATTUNEMENT 125

Means of Attuning 126

Group Participation 134

CHAPTER 9:

THE MAGIC OF THE SHINING ONES 137

Levels of Initiations 142

Realms of Magic Initiation 145

CHAPTER 10:

THE CHALLENGES THAT THE ELVEN ADEPT FACES 155

CHAPTER 11:

RELATING TO THE SHINING ONES 169

Choosing a Master 171

Astrological and Other Influences Of Attraction 173

CHAPTER 12:

MORE ON THE ELVEN STAR AND THE RAYS OF MANIFESTATION 181

CHAPTER 13:

REQUIREMENTS FOR ELVEN ADEPTSHIP AND MASTERY 193

Magical Shift of Consciousness 197

Letting Go of the Small to Attain the Great 201

Using Power 205

Certainty 213

Courage 213

Energy 215

CHAPTER 14:

ASCENDING INTO THE REALMS OF THE SHINING ONES 221

ABOUT THE AUTHORS 235

CHAPTER 1: AWAKENING

While we've often written that faery tales, both ancient and modern, view the faery folk as being ruled by monarchs, this idea is more a reflection of the lives of men and of the world that was and is than a true indication of the Realms of Elfin. This is not to say that there doesn't exist a Hierarchy in Faery, but that it is important to understand that this Hierarchy is a natural one based on real development and merit and not in the least arbitrary or artificially constructed. All hierarchies, organizations and bureaucracies in the world are a pale attempt to recreate, or in many cases bypass or supersede, this natural hierarchy.

The hierarchy of Elfin is a spiritual hierarchy—the hierarchy of illuminated being, of s'elf development of magical maturity—and thus it is the power, of awakened consciousness and expanded and enlightened awareness. Besides the attempts of many to construct this hierarchy in the world, it is also reflected in Nature, where there are hierarchies of intelligence, of knowledge, of personality, beauty, strength, and so forth. While artificial hierarchies tend to be rather strictly structured and unyielding, these natural hierarchies, reflective of the true spiritual hierarchy, are varied and yielding. For instance, while there are general tendencies, we don't all agree about who is most beautiful or most attractive. It is rather like the question, what is your favorite color? It depends on the individual. So, too, the natural hierarchies are, like the true inner hierarchy, dependent greatly on the individual and their own position in the Universe, their individual tendencies.

There is another way that the spiritual hierarchy tends to differ from all artificial hierarchies and even from the hierarchy of

Nature. Artificial hierarchies tend to be pyramid schemes with one or a few people on the top and increasing numbers of individuals in various levels below with the greatest number on the bottom. This formula does not tend to change. The one at the top may change. Sometimes, but rarely one's position on the hierarchy may change, but the structure tends to stay the same. In fact, that is its purpose to reinforce itself and maintain this structure.

On the other hand, while the spiritual hierarchy may have more on the bottom than the top at any particular point, the goal and purpose of this hierarchy is to get everyone at the top, to have everyone progress further and further into the realms of Elfin, the realms of radiant enlightenment.

We might think of it as a game. In the game of the material world the first ones to reach home win; everyone else is considered a loser. In the spiritual game, we gain points when each one reaches home and our ultimate goal is to get everyone home. Then and only then have we truly won the game.

These elves have dedicated most of our lives to uplifting our others. This may seem like selfless service but the truth is it is the only way we can win the game. Only by lifting our kindred up can we ascend. It is that simple. Thus our actions are not selfless, nor selfish, but "s'elfish", which is to say designed to help us by helping others.

The Awakening

Most elfin and otherkin brought up in the world of Man experience what is often called the Awakening. Usually this involves the realization that one is elven, faerie or other, or a variety of other faerie folk, a mixture of elf and pixie, for instance. Most elves go through life feeling different from those around them and alienated from the normal culture anyway. However, though they feel different from most common folk, they often have no idea what they truly are, they just know that they are different until this realization, this awakening, or acceptance comes. We often feel we are not quite human or if human certainly not normal. Normal folk, of course, are eager to remind us of this fact and while at first we often find this reminder of our difference and their lack of acceptance painful, in time we come to embrace their rejection, wearing it as a badge of honor. When we see how they are, how they think, or in most cases, fail to think, we are glad we are not them, although being different has its dangers for they subtly, and too often not so subtly, despise all that is different from them, all who do not eagerly conform.

But this realization, this awakening is not always one of understanding that one is an elf or other. Sometimes, this realization is, in fact, an awakening to the realization that we can in truth be who or whatever we choose to be; that our life and destiny is not shaped by our fate or our genetic history; that we are, indeed, free to be our own s'elves however we choose to define it. This realization stems in part from the understanding that there is a spiritual dimension to our being, that the material world, our ethnic and social history and our genetic lineage do not or need not, entirely define us. We are spirits/souls being born into material bodies and ultimately it is not our body that says who we are, but our spirits. We are elves not because our bodies are descended from elves, but because we choose to be elves; although, it is a basic truth that we choose to be elves because we are elves. (We note here that we may well be descended from elven tribes, such as the Scythians, the Pict-Sidhe or the Tuatha Da Danaan, upon which the tales of elves are mostly based.) In the long run of evolution, we all choose to be who are truly are. We cannot help but do so. We may try to escape our true natures, as so many "normal" folk attempt to do, but in the course of eternity that is a futile quest. We cannot escape our true s'elves.

Nearly every religion attests to the fact that there is a spiritual dimension that exists within, alongside of, and beyond the material world, and yet trapped in this world as we are, where physical pleasure and pain are very real to us, it is sometimes hard to remember this fact, or do more than pay lip service to this idea. But the haunting reality of Death, plus the endless question of where we were before we were conceived, gives pause to the thoughtful about our true condition and the real nature of the Universe.

While some elves and otherkin, in reaction to the scorn they've experienced and suffered in life, often feel they are superior to normal folk, it is important to realize that the underlying spiritual nature of the Universe and the process of evolutionary development applies to all things, all beings in the universe from mineral life, to flora, to animal life, to humanity, to the spirits beyond, from the atom to the constellations, all are in the process of Becoming.

The Sages point out to us that life on Earth and the pleasures, and pains, of this life are transitory. They are an illusion, not because they don't occur but because they don't last. There is within us a hunger for the Eternal, for happiness and pleasure that endures, for love that never fades and is ever true, and for understanding that surpasses all illusion. Life on Earth, being transitory is just another dream that seems so real when we are in the midst of it but which fades, even seems to be forgotten, once it has passed away; although, nothing is ever truly forgotten. We may not remember mentally but our experience is imprinted on our souls forever in the form of the Akashic Record.

Some writers thus picture elves as being immortal beings who never change, but this is not the case. Rather, as spirits we become ever more masterful in both creating and experiencing a changing environment. We don't become perfect and then stay the same, but rather are in a continual state of perfecting and improving ours'elves. We do not become, like Anne Rice's vampires, living statues but rather we evolve into increasingly ephemeral beings of light living in worlds of our own creation.

We do not kill to live or live to kill but live to love and love to live. The death dealers will get exactly the world they've created and so shall we, which is to say that in time death as we know it will die.

Caught up in the world that is, lured by transitory pleasures, or trapped by pain, it is sometimes hard to turn one's mind to the Eternal and even when one realizes our Eternal nature mentally as an idea or concept, it is often difficult to remember it when swept up in the great flood of worldly experience. One must reach beyond the mind, whose function is to question and doubt, and arrive at the heart, and secure there our faith and cling to it. Yet, should one fail in this, and most of us do indeed for lifetimes uncounted fail in this, we need not despair. The true nature of life is evolution whether we remember it or not, whether we have faith or not, its nature remains unchanged and that unchanging nature is one of ever becoming.

What is important to remember is that we shape our lives in all we do. This is our nature; it is our magic; it is our karma. When we act with the Eternal in our minds and hearts, when we come to understand ours'elves as beings who exist in various forms through the ages, we begin to participate in the Life Eternal that is our true state of being and our destiny.

Although our actions shape our lives, ours is not a random Universe. Nor are we the only powers in it. There are laws that govern the Universe and these laws arise naturally out of the Nature of the Universe. They are not arbitrary rules created by some outside power, god, or force but are inherent in the nature of things. One might wonder then do we have any power to shape our lives at all and the answer is quite clearly yes, although at this point for most beings it is a quite limited power. The world we live in is formed by the magics we have created in our past, our karma, which also create our thoughts and philosophies and in this way inform our actions, but it is also created by the magics others have done with whom we've interacted, either positively or negatively, in love or hate, or both, in cooperation or conflict. It is these interwoven spells that have bound us to this world.

We come to understand in time that in order to succeed in the world, to succeed as spirits, we must follow certain percepts, rules, or laws of magic. Again, these are not arbitrary rules but absolutely essential to the evolution of our spirits and our souls. They are the Way we evolve and succeed, become who we truly wish to be, which is to say who we truly are and live as Immortal Spirits in the Eternal Dimensions. We call them therefore the Elven Way.

Some will say that this Way involves the apprehension of what is Good and what is Evil and pursuing the One, or the Other; and that is true in a sense. However, it is probably more accurate to say that this Way delineates what actually works to uplift, liberate and free us from the limitations and confines of this world, what empowers us, as opposed to those things that keep us entangled and bound. Still, to our minds what liberates us and empowers us is good and what binds us and enslaves us is evil, so the difference, while accurate, is subtle.

It may be defined very easily by stating this simple formula: We are free to pursue our own magical creative course as long as we do not obstruct and interfere with others who are doing the same. Clearly, we have the right to defend ours'elves and thus prevent others from interfering with our way, if our way is true, and to prevent them from obstructing others.

We may add to this the fact that in helping others to pursue their true goals, that is find their own true path, we are also de facto aiding our own course. Since we live in an interconnected world, cooperation whenever and wherever possible is always advised and of great benefit to us all. It may also be noted that since we find ours'elves in a world where our magic is limited, mainly by our karma, cooperative action increases the power of our magic. What we cannot accomplish alone we can achieve together.

The Magical Mind

When we speak of going beyond the mind, we do not mean disposing of it entirely or disregarding it. Rather, the idea is to turn the mind into a focused vehicle of our magic, rather than the disorganized anarchy of thoughts it so often tends to be. Thoughts are things, that is they are powers in the world that have potent effects and it is with the focused mind that we obtain true creative power, the power to create our own realms and dimensions of being.

However, when we speak of the power of mind and thought, we don't mean mere ideas. Rather, we are referring to the concentration of consciousness that is empowered by our souls and thus our feelings and passions, supported by our will and our spirit and guided by our purified intention. To create effective magic we must support our spells with our entire being, with our very lives, which means with our every action. To become the great and powerful elven star enchanters we are destined to be, we must integrate our entire being and project it toward the Vision we have seen, felt or even created. The fact that this vision may change from time to time is only to say that to get from here to there we sometimes must take a turn to the right or left. The way is not always straight ahead.

This power of magical consciousness is the power that informs the world. It is the power to create worlds and universes, dimensions and realms of varying type and manifestation. Until we fully obtain this power, which we are destined to do, which we are being groomed to do, we live in the realms of others, just as a child lives in the atmosphere of its parents' home. It is this creative consciousness that has created the universe, however, it is not a thing separate and apart from it, but alive within it. We are part of the body of the creative force. We are in its womb, so to speak. We are truly the Children of the Stars, and like the angels, devas and other spirits, until we obtain the power of Creative Consciousness, we are servants to the great consciousness that bears us within it. We elves often call this Divine Consciousness, Magic.

Here we are not speaking merely of creation in the sense of creating a painting, or writing a book as we do here, but in taking the raw and primordial energy of the Universe and shaping it to one's will and vision. There is no creation of the energy itself. The energy is and is not simultaneously. It is Pure Being and is s'elf existent but utterly unformed and permeable. It is we who through elevation of our consciousness learn to shape it to our will. We do that by becoming ever more the masters of our own fate and destiny, which means learning to guide our thoughts, feelings, and our bodies.

The Elven Star

In a sense we learn to control all these aspects of s'elf at once, but at the same time it is true that we develop these skills, and are given these lessons in various sequences. These aspects of power and being are reflected in the arms/aspects/powers of the extending points of the seven pointed star, our beloved Elf Star that reflects the seven rays of manifestation, the seven root races, the seven sub-races of those root races and the seven basic dimensions attached to the world. We will get into this more later, but for the moment let us note that the creative energy of thought, which is associated with the third arm of the seven pointed star, and thus the third ray, tends to develop as a power in sequence after the development of basic will power of the first ray, and the development of wisdom, thus compassion, with the second ray. These first three rays are the most vital for it is from these that the individual first begins to awaken to hir Divine, which is to say Magical, S'elf and initiates the mastery of hir (his/her) own spirit. To do this, to gain the power of creative magical being, we immerse ours'elves into the material world to develop these powers and obtain mastery over this world, which we accomplish first and foremost through developing mastery over our own s'elves.

Becoming Our Own True S'Elves

One might ask that if we are becoming ours'elves, that is realizing our divine magical elfin nature, then how is it that we aren't already there? How is it that we are not already perfectly ours'elves? How can we not be?

Our perfected being exists in unrealized potential. It means paradoxically that we both exist and don't exist at the same time, this Elven Paradox, like a Zen Koan, is reflected in the nature of the material world where we don't exist, then exist, then don't exist, then exist, etc. And is reflected further in our conscious and unconscious states of being. We are in the process of coming into consciousness. So, too, do we need as Soulful Spirits to descend into the material world, by which we mean the realms of differentiated energy, and to shape it into the dimensions we envision. However, like most things, such as riding a horse, playing a guitar, or doing any other art or craft, our actions are not usually perfect at first. Our skills are limited and thus our creations are seldom what we envision. We come into this world to manifest, or elfin-fest, our perfected s'elves, our true magical, and thus Divine natures and to realize our Vision. We are destined to be god-like beings. Although for we elfin, being elves, that is magical beings living in eternal love and harmony with each other, is quite enough. We do not aspire to be over others, yet the fact is that in shaping the undifferentiated energy of the Universe into form we are indeed assuming responsibility for the energy we use, and its eventual empowerment and realization. All of the Universe is moving toward the realization of its Divine Magical Nature.

To do this we come to distinguish between good and evil, which is to say those things that further us on the Path and those things that obstruct our evolution, development or education. This in great part also means coming to know who we truly are and who and what we are not. The method of doing this is ever by coming to know and trust ours'elves inwardly and to integrate our beings, our conscious and our unconscious, our minds, feelings, bodies and spirits into a unified and powerful consciousness.

The process of this development involves two powerful forces that like two sides of a coin, seem very different but are really part, or are meant to be part, of a consistent whole. These parts are the Soulful nature, which is ever in touch with and longs for relationship with all other being, and the Spirit, which seeks to separate itself in order to distinguish itself or define itself from others. The Spirit seeks its own place in the Universe, while the Soul seeks to have that place be in harmony with all others. On the surface these two seem to be opposites and potentially in conflict but in reality they are not; for if the Spirit finds its true place it will automatic be in harmony with the Universe; and if the Soul is in harmony with the Universe the Spirit easily finds its own place or realm of fulfillment and development. It may sound as though we are finding our place in the great and never changing bureaucracy of the heavens, but in fact we are finding an opening in the Great Dance and moving in harmony and rhythm with the other dancers. The great faerie circle spins round and round creating ever-greater ecstasy.

This process, however, involves two great movements: the first is the *descent* into matter or the clothing of ours'elves with matter in order to learn to form it to our vision. However, because it is in essence dense and not entirely us in our pure form this creates a sort of amnesia. We forget who we truly are, deceived so to speak by the energy we have taken on, and must in a sense persuade this energy to cooperate with us through enlightened leadership. In other words, we need to take care of our bodies, our minds, our feelings, and bring them into harmony with our Vision, which is to say in harmony with our true being.

The second great movement is the gradual realization of this goal, the uniting of this primal energy with our essential natures. And the turning point comes when we awaken to our spiritual nature, the fact and realization as a goal of our Magical S'Elves. Once having done that we set ours'elves upon the path and, while we may at times waver, our kindred the Shining Ones are ever looking out for our best interests.

This first movement is one of becoming individual, of defining ours'elves and involves the struggle for survival, the survival of the body, the survival of one's individual identity. It is here that so often the movement for Mastery is confused with an urge to dominate others.

The second movement involves the realization of our essential connectedness and unity and it is a movement back toward harmonious association. This second movement is often prompted by the first movement, that is to say the need for individual survival pushes us toward working in groups and often the sacrifice of the individual s'elf. The few are sacrificed for the sake of the many and so forth. However, the achievement of security then moves us back toward the first movement of individual power and realization.

The true awakening comes when one realizes that these two forces are not in conflict with each other, but are all part of the great dance. We sway this way and then that. We need others so we can be free to be ours'elves, we need to be strong as individuals so we can help empower and protect our others.

Success in the Universe is found in the Balance, in the Harmony of Opposites. We elves are students of the Tao, the Yin and Yang, from which all things come into being and the way to success is achieved.

The Evolution of Power

When first we seek to rise we tend to do so with the power of the body, the power of force. You will note that ideas concerning magic also follow this hierarchy of development. Star Wars speaks of going with the force and uses the light saber, Harry Potter has wizards and witches with wands shooting bolts of lightning at each other. In the case of Star Wars, the magic of the Jedi involves the mind focused through the directed consciousness of one's feelings and intuition. One "goes with the force", or in modern parlance "goes with the flow." One senses the power and movement of the Universe and acts in harmony with it. In Harry Potter, the magic is primarily mental energy. It is not so much a matter of intuition or the use of one's feelings but of the correct pronunciation of spells. It is vocal. It is the word made flesh. It is in a sense a scientific magic whereas Stars Wars speaks of an artistic or intuitional magic.

These magics are reflected in the world in the form of the camaraderie that can be found in the excited devotees of religious and political movements. It is a great magical power but, like all magic, all power, can be used for good or ill. It is the power that Hitler, Stalin, F. D. Roosevelt and Mao evoked, each in their own way to arouse their followers. (Note while we group these men together because they utilized the same power, we are not saying that they each used it in the same way or with the same intention.) It is this power that invigorates most cults, as well as the power of enlightened spiritual movements. It is the sense of common purpose and unity, and as we say it can and has been used for both good and evil. This is a sixth ray magic, reflected in the second ray but usually evoked by a first ray charismatic personality.

The mental magic is reflected in the great idea or ideal. In many ways, it can be seen in the excitement of scientific discovery. It is the magic of the formula, of the invention, the new and powerful technique and it can, like the feeling/intuitional magic, change people's lives, and like that magic as well it can be used for good or ill. This is true of all magic. It is neither good or bad in itself, it is how it is used in the service of evolution or not that results in good or evil. This is a fifth ray magic, the magic of scientific formula, which is associated also with the third ray of higher mind and enlightened understanding.

What usually evokes these magics, however, is the great magician, the great spirit/individual/singularity/personality who tends to be a charismatic leader. This is first ray magic, although it typically evolves into seventh ray magic. The creative inspiration becomes institutionalized and is taken over by bureaucrats, who typically give it structure so it will endure, and end up structuring it so much that it is eventually strangled to death or collapses under its own weight and inability to change. Almost all great movements, religious, social or political are initiated by these powerful charismatic personalities. This is not the magic of light sabers and shooting wands but of the radiant being who affects people by hir (his/her) mere presence. This is real magical power.

When these powers are combined, that is a first ray charismatic individual evokes the sixth ray devotional feeling and unites it with a third ray great ideal, incredible things occur. However, as we said previously these things can be for the good or for ill and sometimes both.

As we develop as elfin spirits we begin to infuse the second ray of love/wisdom into this magical formula and intent becomes increasingly important. To truly evolve beyond the world of survival/struggle we must set ours'elves toward the illumination not only of ours'elves but all beings and pursue that course steadfastly. Then we may enter the realms of Elfin and take our place among the Shining Ones. Until that occurs, we are ever entangled in the crossfire of contrary magics set in motion by self-serving individuals who seek to dominate others and only care about their own success and have neither compassion nor concern for others. In fact, they ridicule and despise compassion viewing it as weakness. They believe that continual conflict is an unalterable fact of life and in as much as they continue on that course they are quite right, at least for themselves, for they will never rise above it.

While this evocation of the second ray of love/wisdom and thus compassion, seems to be basically a feeling oriented activity, and it is indeed soulful in nature, it comes about through a conscious decision to seek the good, to seek evolution, to pursue change and improvement over stagnation; and it also involves the understanding that what affects one of us affects all of us. We are all interconnected in and through the Magic, which is the Divine Source of all things. The decision to ally ones'elf with the higher forces of nature and evolutionary development also initiates the invocation of the higher mind. One becomes in harmony with the tide of individual spirits who are seeking the same goal and becomes connected to them soulfully. One becomes in essence and in reality one of our elven family, and one's evolution is quickened and aided by those who are further along the same path. Of course, they would not aid us, would not be allowed by the laws of the Universe to do much for us, if we didn't in fact first call out to them for help. The most they can do prior to that is Sing the Songs of Faerie and trust that those who are ready will hear and respond.

In reading about this it may sound like the elf makes a decision toward pursuing the Elven Way, the pursuit of the evolution and enlightenment of all and that the elf's life is changed henceforth. And there is truth to this. One's life does take a decided turn due to this awakening, this illumination. However, it is also true that one's resolve is tested again and again by circumstances and the elf often finds that this resolution toward enlightened behavior must be renewed regularly until it becomes not only a habit but a true part of one's being. At that point one is lifted even higher.

S'elf Sacrifice

It is often said by various spiritual groups that their path requires a good deal of s'elf sacrifice, and in as far as one must consider others and not simply act on one's own behalf, and in as far as the individual must sometimes give up some things that He (she/he) might have gained at the expense of others, this is true. However, it should also be mentioned that for each thing we give up we gain so much more. Think of how much we would be able to invest in education and research if we weren't spending so much money continually building weapons to protect ourselves and our belongings, from those who see themselves as our enemies.

True, others don't instantly become our friends because we have awakened. In fact, certain individuals despise us even more. But we gain the help and support of our kindred both in this world and more particularly in the super-dimensions beyond and the benefits of this cannot be calculated in transitory earthly values. Our elven society extends into dimensions beyond this material world and throughout the Universe.

Higher Mind

This decision, and the action of pursuing this path, awakens the higher mind, or evolved consciousness in the elfin. The fetters of prejudice, discrimination, and enculturated thought fall away leaving one freer to see the world as it truly is and as it can be. This higher mind is not merely a mental mind, a mind of facts, logic and reason, although it is usually far more capable of reasoning than lower minds. It is also a mind of intuitional understanding and creative thought and direct inner knowing. It sees the world more clearly and thus gives one a certain advantage over those who refuse to reason and who cling to prejudice and to the ideas passed down through the ages by their particular social or ethnic group, accepting what they are told to believe without question. Elves are encouraged, even in a way obligated by our natures, to seek truth for ours'elves and to question what we've been told.

Alas, as always, this promotes a conflict in the individual as to how to use superior power and understanding without acting superior over others, which nearly all individuals instinctively hate and resent, nor using it exclusively for one's own benefit or the benefit merely of one's own group or family, tribe, etc. This is no easy task particularly when among those we seek to benefit are the very ones who so adamantly oppose and scorn us. It requires real superiority and it is achieved though time and practice. However, by practicing this higher value of following the superior and enlightened path without acting superior to others, one slowly develops the power of charisma, and this power is the power to transform the world.

This requires the development of modesty, a magical technique that leads in time to the power of humility. It demands the sacrifice of one's personal ego, which can be difficult at first when the elf is endeavoring with great effort to overcome the projections of inadequacy that the dominant culture has foisted upon hir (him/her) in attempt to force the elf into conformity. Thus this sacrifice is a great one and it takes incredible mastery to remain humble or modest when the recognition one has so painfully missed is finally offered to one. But again this sacrifice is rewarded by those who will uplift one, for modesty is ever lifted up and supported in the world, while those who seize their glory and boast of their accomplishments encounter always those who would tear them down. The Universe seeks balance in all things and when the lowly are modest they are uplifted and when the great are modest they are supported. This is a subtle and cunning magic that should not be underestimated although only the true initiate understands this.

Elven Sages

To remind us ever of this need to rise up and lift our others with us, to have compassion for others even those who oppose us, to endeavor to understand the true natures and motivations not only of ours'elves but all others, the Shining Ones send us Sages who appear in many forms, in nearly all cultures and speak though various social and religious philosophies encouraging us to strive toward the light, to seek ever the good of all, and to further evolution in all that we do. We elves call this the Way of the Fair or the Elven Way.

Though these sages do not always, perhaps seldom at this point consider thems'elves to be elves, we elves always welcome the true sage among us. Whatever they may call thems'elves, whether Christian, Buddhist, Moslem, Hebrew, Sikh or whatever, if they are a true sage offering the true light they are elven enough to us. While elves tend to love costumes, we don't judge individuals by their clothes, or the trappings of their religion, but by the power and content of their souls and spirits. Thus while we listen to the messages that a sage may bring us for its truth and relevance to our lives, we must confess we also judge the sage by hir own ability to live up to the teachings sHe espouses; although, we elves tend to be easy in our evaluations, as any who have taken classes from us can avow, and we know that the truth can come even from imperfect beings. In fact, what else are we likely to encounter in the material world?

In heeding the wisdom of these sages, and in realizing that wisdom, that is in making it real in our own lives by manifesting it through our actions day by day, we become like them and we rise on the path of spiritual evolution and become living examples of enlightenment; and eventually we, too, become the sages unto others passing on the wisdom that has uplifted us. We translate all teachings into our own elven understanding and thus in simple ways we bring our faerie magic into the world.

Evolution: Spiritual and Mundane

In this current era, when most folks view the world, view the tales of elves, even think of gods or god, they do so from a materialistic point of view. Evolution is seen or denied in terms of the development of the physical body of man and animals. The numerous movies and television shows about advanced mutant humans with exceptional powers reflect this idea that evolution primarily involves a physical or genetic change. There are Darwin's and other's theories that we evolved with the apes from common ancestors.

However, when we write here of evolution, we primarily mean spiritual evolution: the evolution and enlightenment of the soul and spirit of a being that lifts it from normalcy into an awakened understanding of life. In its simplest form evolution is education. It involves the development of one's mind, the maturity of one's feelings and interactions, the instilling of one's spirit with courage, perseverance and other noble virtues. The more we develop ours'elves as individuals the more powerful and evolved we become. When that development involves a dedication to doing what is fair for all it becomes soulful and thus true spiritual development. This is the Elven Way and it leads us to the Starlight Path of the Shining Ones.

While the materialistic point of view almost demands that one's DNA must mutate in order to activate higher powers, the elven sages know that it is usually the other way around. It is the development of the spiritual soulful being that in time affects the vibration of the individual, brings enlightenment and transforms or mutates one's DNA. It is true there are certain techniques such as meditation and various shamanic practices that can alter the synaptic structure of the brain and thus change one's life and nature. But usually before anyone engages in those activities, sHe (she/he) must have heard the call of the soul and the spirit. The soul calls one to develop one's compassion, fairness, and loving connection, while the spirit calls one to achieve personal success, power and individual style. By interweaving these two goals, we increase ours'elves as magical spiritual beings, awakening the Divinity within us, and in time altering our very bodies. We evolve as soulful spirits, as elves we become ever more powerful, intelligent and mature and thus increasingly able to cooperate with others, find our true place in the Universe, and become all we wish to be.

The Path is never-ending, the Way is ever before us, the Choice is always now, and we are eternally evolving. This is the Elven Way.

MAKING EACH DAY A BLESSING
MAKING EVERY NIGHT A GRACE
BREATHING THE LIGHT OF ELF MAGIC
RUSHING TO LOVE'S WARM EMBRACE
NOURISHED BY THE SMILES OF OUR KINDRED
TAUGHT BY THE WAYS OF THE WISE
LED BY THE SOULS INDEPENDENT
THUS DO WE EACH REALIZE
THE PATH THAT WE TREAD IS UNENDING
THE FOREST IT GROWS EVER NEW
THE LIGHT OF THE TREES DOTH SURROUND US
THE STORIES OF FAERIE ARE TRUE
INHERITED WE OUR ENCHANTMENT
FROM SHINING ONES ANCIENT AND FAE
PASSED FROM THIS WORLD INTO LEGEND
WHAT THEY ONCE WERE, WE'RE TODAY

CHAPTER 2:
STEPPING ONTO THE PATH

The first step upon the path, as we've already mentioned, is the Awakening. One must first realize there is a path before one can begin to consciously tread it. This awakening is prompted by our need to gain some power and mastery over our lives and the circumstances of our lives, and the realization that the transitory pleasures of the world do not bring true inner happiness. Even those who achieve all they desire in the world most often find there is something missing; something more they want; something that they can't buy, borrow or steal. That something more is usually found both in a greater understanding of the spiritual nature of life, but in the attainment of purpose and meaning.

So the second step upon the path is that attainment. We see the greater Vision, we understand the Way, and we dedicate ours'elves toward the fulfillment of the great Vision/Purpose, which is the evolution of the individual and the species and in time all of life toward the realization of its Divine Magical Nature. That is to say the realization of the Universe as a miraculous magical event.

The realization of purpose or meaning in life is an immense power. Even when it functions with limited understanding, as it does in separative religions and cults, or in nationalistic patriotic movements that set their own group over others, it is incredibly powerful. And the individuals, although they seldom realize their individuality in these cases and in fact are often encouraged to sacrifice their individuality for the sake of the group, who are caught up in this sense of purpose are enthused about life and filled with energy. It is a potent power, indeed. When it is combined, as it eventually must be with the soulful realization of our interconnectedness and our relationship to all things, and the realization that what affects each of us in time affects us all, it becomes even more powerful. One at this point enters not only a vast and far-reaching spiritual frasority (combining the words fraternity and sorority) but is also supported by the Nature of the Universe and the Magic itself. One is in harmony with and moving with the flow of the Universe and that increases one's magical power multifold.

Alas, in taking these first two steps upon the path, one's magical development is inevitably quickened. This quickening prompts the attention of the Lords of Karma, those spirits whose duty it is to assist one in purifying ones'elf so one becomes a powerful instrument of the great purpose. What is the great purpose? The liberation of the individual from the chains of ignorance and the karma it provokes.

Of course, karma must always be balanced, but in the lives of most individuals this is often a slow process, taking place in the form of a readjustment from one life to another. But the aspirant upon the path, the new initiate into the Elven Way, understands that negative karma is a bar to obtaining the magical power sHe (she/he) needs to realize hir (his/her) goals and to fulfill hir purpose in life. Thus the elf takes a most important action, which is consciously ceasing to create new negative karma, and endeavoring in as much as possible to overcome any karma in the form of debts owed from the past. It is this second movement that the Lords of Karma take note of, and assist us by sending challenges that if accomplished will help free us from these burdens, debts and chains of past actions. This effort to clear one's karma and particularly to crease creating new obligations is the third step upon the path.

The fourth step is a very personal step. It is a movement of spirit and involves the realization of the elf as an individual, of one's true nature, individual propensities, abilities, talents, and goals. This fourth step leads to the development of personal style, which evolves naturally from the development of the individual spirit.

To do this the elf must come to understand hir own nature, hir weaknesses, hir propensities, hir strengths, hir goals and hir desires. One usually proceeds by increasing one's talents and abilities, but it is also often wise to make at least small efforts to strengthen ones'elf in the areas where one is lacking, to overcome one's limitations and weaknesses. Some will be more energetic about this than others and each must decide for hir own s'elf whether it is more important to put most of one's energy toward what one is already good at doing and becoming even better at it or toward eliminating one's weaknesses. However, it is important to understand that you are who you are for a reason and in pursuing your goals with the greater Vision in mind and an enlightened understanding of one's connection to the all of life, one is free to pursue whatever Path one chooses. It is the pursuit of those immediate desires, the desires that concern one in a particular lifetime or period in life that leads us inevitably to confront our limitations that stand in the way of achieving those goals and to developing our skills that further our success. We need not eschew the immediate for the infinite; however, the realization that the mundane resides within the infinite gives life greater perspective.

Therefore, do all you can to improve yours'elf in every way you can. Keep the vast in mind, but act in the Here and Now. The saying: "Think Globally, Act Locally" is very much in keeping with this aspect of spiritual development. You have every right to be yours'elf. In fact, the purpose of spiritual evolution is the perfection of your and every other individual's, unique s'elfhood; the realization of what many folks call your individual godhead within, but which we elves call your Divine Magic.

The fifth step is the establishment of compassion as a permanent aspect of mind. Compassion, and the view to seeing things from other's point of view as well as one's own, must become a habit of consciousness. This is a soulful realization, the understanding that we are connected to all things, and as one gains this wider view of life one is able to both see and affect changes, thus magic, on an ever widening and more expansive scale. One thinks Globally, Solar-ly, Galactic-ly, Inter-Galactic-ly, ever outward toward Universal Cosmic Consciousness.

While this begins from an aspect of s'elf interest, that is one comes to understand that all one does affects others, and that eventually in the form of karma it returns to ones'elf; in time this Cosmic Understanding leads one toward increasing power and therefore greater responsibility on a vaster scale of development. As this happens, one enters the realms of the Shining Ones and begins to advance in the hierarchies of those who guide and nurture the development of life through the Root Races and the evolution of the species of a particular world, globe, and/or dimension.

The Shining Ones were once where we are. They have evolved in earlier cycles of evolution to reach the level they currently hold, and we in time will replace them as they develop further. The process goes ever on. We become more and more powerful as we evolve, more and more of what we wish to be. We are actualizing our potential and as we do so we cross the dimensions getting closer and closer to Faerie, the realm that is the heart of the Divine and Sacred Magic.

Placing one's s'elf upon the Path, one immediately draws the attention of the Shining Ones who will thenceforth ever seek to guide and send the signs, omens, and magic needed to achieve one's goals as an elfin spirit, to fulfill one's soul's purpose, which is loving and harmonious union with Nature and the all of the Universe, and to steadily and surely increase one's powers so one becomes ever more successful in a fashion that doesn't accumulate negative, thus limiting karma, and which benefits the individual elf and all others.

The Elven Way

The Elven Way is straight and narrow
As it twists and winds
Up and down and all around
Its path it ever finds
Through the mountains
Cross the streams
By the bracken thick
Weaving mid the forest gloom
And across the concrete quick
On mossy down, in caverns deep
We follow our true star
And ever seek our kindred true
Both near and those afar
And when we find each other
We share a tender laugh
Before we venture on again
On this Eternal Path.

CHAPTER 3:
ESOTERIC EDUCATION

As the elf begins to pursue the Elven Way, the Shining Ones take note and actively seek to educate the elf's spirit. This education takes place in the form of life events that challenge one, what is often called the School of Hard Knocks, but also one begins to study in the esoteric school that these elves call the University of the Unseen. The Shining Ones speak to us through our dreams and our intuitions and our inner hunger to unite with Faerie. These lessons filter into our waking consciousness as flashes of memory, glimpses of dreams and an instinctual sense of direction. All exoteric education is merely a reflection of this inner training, just as all ceremonies of initiation are merely a symbol of the true inner initiation.

It is most often the case that before an individual begins hir outer education or search into the realms of magic, mysticism and faerie reality, sHe has been prompted by the Shining Ones, thus heard the call of Elfin. And while the individual doesn't always, perhaps seldom, consciously remember this Call, hir soul cannot forget it. It haunts hir like a name on the edge of hir consciousness that sHe can't quite call to mind, but which is on the tip of hir tongue, and it becomes in time like a song sHe has heard that sHe can't get out of hir head.

While not all people remember their dreams, and few, if any of us, remember all of our dreams, the more attuned to Elfin we become the more important our dreams become to us and the more frequently we tend to remember them, as well as, see them as an important part of our lives. It is true that not all our dreams are significant dreams, anymore than all our conversations are about important topics, but certain dreams are quite important, are in fact messages from Faerie and the

Shining Ones and these tend, as we progress upon the Path, to be more easily remembered. They stand out. Sometimes, in fact, they are sent in the form of nightmares, just to be sure we wake up and remember them. For that is what a nightmare usually says, "Wake up and remember me."

In time, our dreams and our waking reality begin to blend together. It is not that one cannot tell them apart, but mundane life starts to take on a more dreamlike quality as the realms of Faerie and the normal world overlap. We are able to see both the world as it presents itself and the spiritual dimension, the Faerie reality that lies behind it. At this point, we are able to not only see faeries, and other beings, in their ephemeral states of being, but also see those of faerie nature who are cloaked in the energy of the material world and who appear for the most part to be quite mundane to most folk, or merely dismissed as being weird, but who radiate powerful magical energy. One begins to *see*, that is gains *the Sight*; and a wider range of possibility opens to the elf.

Usually, at this point in the magician's education, sHe also feverously consumes various esoteric and magical texts, according to hir personal interests and propensities. Many of these texts are repetitive, however, in time the aspiring magician/mystic/witch/sorcerer/yogi realizes that such reminders of the path are immensely helpful and one seeks more and more of them. For the elves in particular these esoteric metaphysical teachings can be found in fiction as well as non-fiction, even in movies and televisions shows. We consume it all seeking the germ of truth and inspiration in each and every one of them.

And more than that, we begin to experiment. We are not passive students who merely listen and practice rote memorization in hopes of spouting facts that make us sound like experts on the occult. We are practitioners, researchers, ever seeking the spells, glyphs, spirits and other bits of magic that work for us and can make our lives more successful. We elves, however, are not inclined to strictly follow one system. We mix and match, being by nature eclectic. There are some who would warn us against doing such. But there are also those who with trembling voices try to scare us from doing magic at all. We, however, are under the guidance of the Shining Ones and as long as we follow the basic percepts of pursuing our own way without hindering others, we have nothing really to fear, although, it is still often wise to keep our magic and our elfin natures hidden from certain folk who are as yet not ready to know the truth, and who despise all that is different from them.

The Shining Ones expect us to experiment with magic. While it is true there are certain limitations placed upon us by karma, which is also the limit of our personal development and is mostly for our own safety, we are wise to experiment, like research scientists of the occult. Our primary lessons, however, are not about spells and spirits, although we may certainly encounter or study these, but about the development and control over our own s'elves, our personal vehicles for magic, which are our minds, feelings, and our actions and intentions/motivations. Everything we do exoterically or esoterically to improve our capacity to use these vehicles effectively are to our benefit and we are aided in this quest, through hints, suggestions and synchronistic events by the Shining Ones.

We develop our minds by learning to reason, use logic, discriminate fact from falsehood, but also by learning to focus the mind and concentrate it upon our goal. We improve the power of our feeling body by calming our souls, and awakening compassion within us so we sense our association with all things, which is our means of affecting magic. We cannot affect anything with which we do not have a connection, after all. We also establish control over our desires and reactions so we use them as a directional guide and cannot be manipulated by others attempting to provoke us. It is we who control our desires. Not our desires that control us. It is we who formulate our reactions, rather than being prone to automatic or knee-jerk responses that others can use to manipulate us.

The third aspect of development is the gaining of power over our actions, which includes not only clarifying our thoughts and goals, and attaining mastery over our reactions, but also in making sure our intentions are in keeping with our soulful and spiritual vision. Our intent to be Fair in all things is a primary aspect of Elfin magic. We are the Fair Folk not only because we are thought to be beautiful but also because we seek what is right and fair in all situations. When individuals are in tune with their natural and original state of innocence they become in harmony with the Universe and with all beings of a higher order, and they instinctively support what is fair and just. It is true that this innocence is often lost or tarnished as one progresses through the world, and not all folks act fairly, in fact most do not. But that does not alter the fact that at the heart of the Universe, balance and fairness are equated and the Universe ever seeks balance.

Of course, individuals are each at their particular level of development, which also alters from life to life. Just as there are those, like the Shining Ones, who have evolved beyond us, there are also those who are developing at levels that are not as advanced as we currently are, and we, like the Shining Ones, begin to have increasing responsibility for noting their position and helping them on their own level as best we may.

In each lifetime, we first recapitulate in an encapsulated form all that we went through previously in order to arrive at the point we currently are and proceed from there. As we progress as spirits, our first true spiritual Awakening is reflected again and again in each successive lifetime at an earlier age. Also, the earlier we awaken in this life the sooner we can progress onward. But the essential thing we come to understand is that we have the power over our own destiny. That is to say that it is only our own s'elves who can cease creating the limitations of karma for us, and only our own s'elves, no matter how much help and grace we receive from the Shining Ones, the devas, and the angelic beings, who can put in the energy and effort toward positive realization and progress on our path.

Besides our karma, that is the limitations placed upon us from past deeds/magic, there is also our fate, which is a form of karma that involves the realization that we are only as advanced as we currently are, but also involves the limitations placed upon us by the responsibilities and relationships we have undertaken relative to others. This is our karma, too, although it is good to remember for the most part this is karma that we have willingly undertaken though relationships and obligations initiated in previous lives. This is about soulful connection. There comes a time in an elf's life when sHe can progress to other dimensions and must choose to abandon those sHe has come to love and go on without them or stay behind and await and help their evolution. It is a free choice that each of us makes in time and it is a true test of our love. However, whether one moves on or not, the path does not change, one still progresses toward s'elf realization as long as one continues to strive.

As one begins to see behind the world of appearances, one develops a certain amount of detachment. The artificial dramas and struggles that so many folk mistake for life and excitement no longer move the elf. This "soap opera" life is not for us. We seek a deeper and more profound connection to Life and all within it. We become calmer and increasingly able to stand in the still eye of the storm. We become devoted and dedicated to our one true purpose, which is the realization of our true magical natures, and to that same development in our kindred, and all other things are made to serve that purpose. The more we evolve soulfully, the more we realize that all beings in the Universe are our kindred, that is to say: we are related to everything either directly or indirectly.

While this primary desire, this *Silver Flame of Elfland* is the primary passion of our souls, and while we become increasingly detached from the lure of worldly pleasure, that does not mean that we are unfeeling beings or inured to pleasure, nor that we necessarily pursue the path of asceticism. We elves enjoy life to its fullest and appreciate the wonder and beauty of living and the pleasures that material life offers us, but we don't let these pleasures control us. Elves avoid addictions of all kinds, and we are not inclined toward s'elf indulgence, except upon occasion. We never wish to become the slaves to habit.

Our deepest passion, besides the realization of our true s'elves, is ever our connection to our kindred. The drive toward personal magical realization is the goal of our spirit, the increasingly deepened connection to our beloved is the goal of our soul, in time we come to understand that these two drives function in concert and support each other, as we ours'elves support our kindred in their own quest toward individual realization and they support us in ours. We love them for who they truly are and wish them to be totally successful in their own s'elves. They hold the same desire for us.

Magical Sacrifice

All achievement requires effort. It may also require sacrifice. However, when we speak of sacrifice we don't mean the killing of animals, or even the offering of your own blood in a chalice. We are speaking of the very real and voluntary sacrifices one chooses to make in life to protect and promote what is good and right from the wicked and destructive. When soldiers sacrifice being with their families and loved ones to go off to war to protect their country and those they cherish — that is real sacrifice. And they may very well, and often do, sacrifice their blood, their life or limbs in doing so.

However, most sacrifice is not so extreme and involves the little things of life, the day to day sacrifices one makes when one gives up that candy bar because they wish to lose weight, or doesn't go out to party so they can stay home and study and improve their knowledge and their lives. So, too, do we give up what is near for what is afar, sacrificing immediate gains for long term rewards, postponing immediate gratification so we may grow stronger and more powerful in time. These little sacrifices, while small, add up and what we give up in temporary pleasure we gain in the satisfaction of being stronger spirits and personalities.

However, these sacrifices are best when they are meaningful. Denying ours'elves merely to deny our bodies without any purpose is contrary to our natures and will in time provoke the rebellion of the body and our unconscious. All things that do not bring the states of our being into harmony will in time instigate internal conflict, which is the opposite of what we wish to achieve. When we limit the pleasure of the body we are wisest to do so in a way that not only increases our willpower but is of positive and long lasting value in terms of health or attractiveness, thus emotional/feeling satisfaction, for the body as well. The same is true for our minds, spirits and souls. A bit of indulgence here and there helps balance our intense devotion to the Vision. The elf, hirs'elf, must ever be the judge of what is best for hir.

Going One's Way

Alas, although we may sacrifice for the greater good, do what we do for our friends and loved ones, that doesn't mean that they will understand what we are doing. In fact, often when one puts one's foot upon the Path, begins to tread the Elven Way, those who seemed closest to us are shocked by this change in our behavior and character. They, naturally, want us to remain as we are. After all, that's who they've come to love and relate to.

The elf, for hir part, is often shocked by this lack of response from hir others. Having awakened. Having seen the Vision. SHe naturally wishes to share this great revelation with those sHe loves most. Alas, these individuals, not having awakened thems'elves, seldom respond well to this attempt to persuade them, and often a distance opens up between the elf and hir friends. In time, the elf understands this fact and realizes that different spirits awaken at different times, have different paths, and come to the Way each in their own time. SHe (she/he) ceases to expect sudden transformation of the individuals sHe loves and begins to deals with these individuals on the level that their spirits are at the time. SHe doesn't expect each individual will understand what sHe has realized, nor share hir path, but sHe does demand a respect for hir and hir path, for if that is not forthcoming the relationship will surely cease. We elves are friends with all sorts of folks, elves and other, man, woman, and varieties myriad. In fact, the Elven Way is the way of friendship, but it is also the way of mutual respect and appreciation.

In the early stages however, the elf is often forced to decide between pursuing the Way and losing friends because of it, or giving up the Way and gaining or retaining acceptance. Elves, by nature, tend to choose freedom over acceptance and once one has truly seen the Way, it is difficult to go back. And wisdom and experience tell us that all such friendships are temporary anyway when they are not aligned with the Eternal Pursuit of Magical Spiritual Realization.

Thus the elf is often forced to sacrifice friendships that sHe cherished. Not because sHe wishes to end the friendship but because the "friend" simply cannot accept the evolution of the elf. However, while elves will sacrifice many things to progress on the path, we never sacrifice our true ideals nor our souls, which is to say that while we may wane at times from pursuing the path, once awakened we can never really give up the path of evolution of our true s'elves, for to do so is to lose our spirit; and we can never give up our compassion and sense of fairness toward all other beings, for to do that is to lose our souls. Life and circumstances require us to be flexible at times, and we may find we have to make many compromises to get by, but

The Elven Way

even then there are things that we hold in the depth of our beings, and to give them up is to lose our very s'elfhood. Fortunately, we elves are some of the most flexible and adaptable beings in the Universe and as we evolve as elven spirits, we become increasingly more so.

And though we hunger to succeed in the world as much as anyone, elves discover that we cannot compromise our principles concerning the treatment of the Earth. Thus we are sometimes at a disadvantage to those who don't mind polluting the earth for their own profit, or taking advantage of others in order to get ahead. Ever we are guided by what is best for our own s'elves and all others. While we must at times sacrifice what is near, we gain what is afar, for we look ever to the Eternal and ever seek to do what will create a better world for all and to reunite the mundane world with the magical realms of Faerie so that the material realm comes to express its true magical nature. It many ways the world is like a diamond that has become covered in mud. We are here to clean it up and polish it.

Often much is sacrificed in the short run of things, and the elfin often finds hirs'elf subject to the prejudices of others. Even when they don't know sHe is an elf, *normal* folk often still sense and frequently resent hir individuality and hir courage in being hir own s'elf, for it reminds them of their own inner lack of courage. However, all such sacrifices are in time rewarded with increased powers and even those who seem to oppose us on the surface often support us in the depth of their souls, for they too hunger to realize their own true natures and even while criticizing our independence they cannot help but hold a secret, begrudged admiration for the elven and a wish that we succeed. Deep within they come to sense that our success is their success as well. And it is good to remember that while there are those who oppose us from time to time, in the long run we are only limited by our own abilities and as we seek to increase and improve these, we become ever freer as spirits and ever more powerful as enchanters. The greatest struggle we face is not between us and those who interfere with, or criticize, us but between our spirit, which seeks ever to become greater and more powerful as an individual, and our soul that hungers for union and communion with others. Always it is we as free and individual spirits that must decide the degree and limits of our responsibility to others, keeping in mind that nearly everything we wish in the world beyond our own s'elves, is to be found and achieved though them.

One might think that our increasing devotion to the Way would make us into humorless fanatics. But quite the opposite is true. The further we progress upon the Way, the more flexible and adaptable we become. We develop a compassion for the failings and limitations of others, principally because we know that we were once where they are now, struggling as they do, and we understand. We really do. And we develop a true sense of the absurdity of life. We do laugh at others and their follies, but mostly because they remind us of our own follies and we can't help but laugh, as well as moan sometimes, at all the foolish things we have done through the lifetimes. In fact, one of the sure signs of progress in elfin magic and in spiritual development is that the individual demonstrates an increasing appreciation for the humorous side of life.

This does not mean we don't take our path seriously, but the further we evolve the more we become and hold all things in balance. We take our sense of humor seriously. We hold our devotion lightly in our hearts. We move from the place of calm and strive to remain calm in all movement. The deeper we penetrate into Faerie, the more comfortable we become with paradox. We are perfectly ours'elves at all times, yet ever becoming. We are modest about our powers, and powerful in our modesty. We are independent spirits in harmony with the Great Plan. We are elves.

Service

In time, sacrifice becomes service. We cease needing to give things up and instead we devote our time and energy toward the realization of the Elven Way. We find our place in the Universe, the place that is destined for us by the uniqueness of our own natures. And we devote ours'elves to helping our others toward the realization of their own natures. These things are interconnected. The greater we become, the more responsibility we have for others; the more responsibility we assume for our others, the greater we become. The actualization of our Divine Magical Natures involves both the realization of ours'elves as unique spirits and the increasingly harmonious interconnection with the all of life. Just as all sacrifice must be voluntary to be true sacrifice so, too, does genuine service need to be voluntarily offered to fully activate the power that comes from such service. Any resistance is an obstacle to the benefits one will accrue from one's service. It is important to understand our interconnection. To be utterly alone and disconnected in the Universe is to become so isolated and karma bound that one is totally limited by one's own determination to be separate from all things other.

Some elves, in fact quite a few, have wearied of the world and all the suffering that goes on here. We often feel powerless to do anything about it. Famine, war, pollution, greed, just plain petty cruelty on a day-to-day basis committed by folks who claim to be holier than thou, drives us insane. Some desire to escape the world into Faerie. Some feel like giving up. But the truth is, this is the fate, the geas, quest, obligation that is upon us. The dark magics are the very thing we have come to master and overcome. And while what we do often seems unimportant, achieving very little at all that, too, is just the voice of wicked spells trying to convince us to give up and not do anything, that all our efforts are wasted and hopeless, and it is useless and meaningless to try to change anything. They tell us it doesn't really matter what we do, or if we do anything at all, because things never change.

The more the elf awakens, the more clearly the elf sees these dark spells for what they truly are. What we do may be small, but all our magics count, no matter how small. Every effort we put forth does make a difference in our own lives, and in the lives of our kindred, if nothing else. We are creating our own realms of Elfin in everything we do and the magic we do is important. It is true that at some point some of us will go on to Faerie, while those who have so persistently created evil in the world and pursued the path of wickedness will inherit the world they've created. In time, we will each find our own place. We are not all powerful. We can but do our best, but in doing our best we become the best we can be and the realms of Faerie unfold before us.

> "WE ELVES AND FAERIES ARE OFTEN PORTRAYED AS DANCING IN A CIRCLE. THIS IS BOTH BECAUSE WE SEE LIFE AS A DANCE AND BECAUSE THE ELVEN WAY GOES EVER ON."
> —THE SILVER ELVES

The Elven Way

My faults I find
Make me inclined
To ever do them over
Repeating every folly
Like I'm rolling round in clover
But then my love
So sweet and kind
Does whisper in my ear
And I do find I better mind
For the one I hold so dear
For this is what the elven do
They accept you as you are
And loving thus you feel you must
Be better then by far.

CHAPTER 4:
THE SHIELD OF NORMALCY

Most elves come into the world and discover at a very early age that we are different than most of those around us. This is an indication that the elf awakened to their magical nature in a previous lifetime and is quick to sense that sHe is not quite like the mass of humanity. Often, because of this the elf is scorned or rejected by those who resent the fact that sHe does not conform, has the courage not to conform, and they bully hir because of it. The elf in reaction to this scorn, teasing and bullying frequently comes to hate these folk in turn.

Alas, this hate is a subjective attachment that links the elf to those sHe hates in a negative fashion and which not only obstructs hir magic, but drains hir magical energy from hir, which is to say that the energy used to hate those others is, in fact, wasted energy that could and would be better spent in a positive effort to realize one's soulful spiritual magical nature. Don't waste your energy struggling with those who are negative, that's what they want. They want you to be entangled and trapped into a negative relationship with them; instead of continuing your development of your own s'elf and your powers, and forging onward toward Elfin. By doing this, you circumvent their magic, rendering it powerless and therefore a waste of their own time and energy.

It might be helpful to understand that the enculturation that is instilled in the mass of folk in order to promote the idea and value of being normal is not merely an effect of dark magic. It is true that when this enculturation promotes hatred for those who are different that it is, indeed, a dark magic spell, but most enculturation, which makes being normal seem to be a positive thing, and which convinces the individual to fit in to society, and that things like elves and magic don't really exist, is created as a protection for these individuals who otherwise would be overwhelmed by the *reality of Reality*; and who are, as yet, unprepared to live within or even acknowledge the existence of the Perilous Realms of Faerie, where magic is real, dreams do come true, but nightmares also threaten. We must be strong within ours'elves and powerful in our magics to wander there unescorted.

It is unwise in most cases to try to convince these individuals of the reality of our elven natures, or the reality of magic. If they do encounter things that they cannot explain within their worldview, their minds quickly erase the memory of these encounters, so that even in moments when they are reminded of the experience, they question whether it ever really happened at all. They are not meant to acknowledge these things as yet and it is good for the elf to realize that they are, spiritual speaking, rather like children for whom knowing certain things would prove either incomprehensible or potentially dangerous. They are, in effect, shielded by their own psyches.

Taking the Gates of Heaven By Storm

Some individuals speak of taking the Gates of Heaven by Storm. In a sense this can occur when one takes certain psychedelics that provide insight, revelation and expansion of consciousness. However, these shamanic tools, while helpful to the initiate, only give one a glimpse of that greater reality, a peek into Faerie. They cannot transport one there permanently. It is only one's effort, on a day-to-day basis, to develop ones'elf and one's magic by which one will acquire the key, the secret formula of being that will allow one to remain in those Magical Dimensions.

Alas, the opposite is not the case. Some can in fact take the Gates of Hell by Storm and wind up being a permanent resident. In many cases, the use of certain drugs or alcohol will bypass the psychic barriers that protect the individual and this can have devastating consequences both for them and for others. Some might say that the use of these drugs opens up the portal to the spirit worlds, although we elves see the drugs themselves as being spirits. When you imbibe the drug you are taking the spirit within you. You are inviting that spirit into your consciousness.

So if you can *Take the Gates of Hell by Storm*, why can't you *Take the Gates of Heaven by Storm*? The difference is between sex and true love. One can't force another to truly love hir, the Gates of Heaven, but one can buy sex, the Gates of Hell. It is easy to fall and so much harder to rise up.

How do you tell which spirits will lead you to Heaven or Hell, or really to the various dimensions of Faerie that contain places that are wondrous and places that are terrifying? Usually, but not always the difference can be found in how addictive the drug/spirit is or how destructive to one's body. The more likely the drug is to be addictive, the more that spirit is inclined to enslave you and lead you eventually to hell-scapes. However, even non-addictive spirits who frequently bring enlightenment and revelation can be dangerous for those who are not ready to those revelations. Some folks are not ready to know the truth. If you try to tell them those things they don't really wish to know, they will stick their fingers in their ears and babble, blah, blah, blah, blah. It is a mantra/chant/spell for invoking ignorance.

Ever the truth comes back to this, no matter what help the spirits may give you, no matter what the spirits may offer you or reveal to you, it is always you who must put forth the effort to progress on the path. No one can tread the Elven Way for you. Many, however, are on the path with you, some kindred are ahead, some are behind, and some beside you. Connecting with them is truly the way and makes the path so much easier.

A few folks, not many, but some, upon having the spirits reveal the realms of Faerie to them, are driven insane, at least for a while. They are unprepared for the revelation of the more expansive world that is reality and they are for a spell thrown in conflict with the world, and the worldview, that they had previously accepted as true. All we can say to those who wish to summon these spirits to aid in their magic, is that one, they should avoid spirits that seek to enslave them, and two, that they be certain they are ready for such an adventure, that the time is right, and they are among those that they trust.

Alcohol, which is commonly and quite accurately referred to as Spirits, or alcoholic spirits, is a spirit that can go either way. For some, this spirit can be addictive, for others if used in moderation it can be a social delight, a good and convivial companion. Again, the elfin magician must decide for hir own s'elf how involved will be hir relationship with this spirit. However, while the alcoholic spirits can be pleasant companions from time to time, it is seldom that they bring real revelation. And note that if one summons them often they will want to come back again and again. Also, the more your invoke them, the more they tend to wander about in your subconscious, in time opening doors that should not be opened until you are really ready or they will evoke spells that summon more spirits, often quite violent and spiteful ones. At that point, one has lost control of one's life and magic and falls under the power of these spirits. You do not need, nor is it really wise, to be authoritarian with the spirits. But neither do you ever wish these spirits to gain control over you. This is a path of mastering your own spirit.

There are certain individuals due to a chemical imbalance in their bodies, or because of tremendous stress in their lives, *naturally* see spirits without the use of drugs. When these spirits are of a lower order and the individual is unprepared for dealing with them, we tend to call these individuals schizophrenic. When the individual is an evolved being who does not lose control over their own spirit, or take the babblings of lower spirits too seriously, we tend to call these individuals "schizophonic," psychic or elves. Unfortunately, those individuals who we call insane that are plagued by demons in their consciousness also often tend to attract demons in the material world so there are, all too often, unfortunate cases of cruelty toward these individuals by those who should be looking after them.

Raising One's Shield

The enculturation and other protections that shield the normal folk from the realization of other dimensions are lifted when the elf steps upon the path and begins to tread the Elven Way. The elf, as any other initiate, increasingly assumes responsibility for hir own protection from negative psychic forces. This does not mean our kindred of higher orders don't aid us, but they expect us to become more and more proficient in setting the wards and protections of our own magic circle, which is to say our own consciousness.

Naturally enough, the dark forces will seek to assail the elf even more, both in the form of temptations and in more direct psychic assaults that manifests as doubts and fears. The Shining Ones and our especial guardians allow this because it is in just this way that we become increasingly proficient at protecting ours'elves. It is the destiny of each elf to gain mastery over all the spirits in hir realm. This does not mean we control them absolutely. We are not tyrants, but we do assume increasing responsibility for influencing them and making sure that they observe the guidelines we set forth for interaction and functioning in our area of manifestation. There is an expectation of harmonious association that is necessary for the proper function of the realms over which we hold sway.

As we say these lower spirits tend to function in two ways. They tempt us to use our powers selfishly, with no regard or compassion for others, thus moving us toward soullessness, or they simply disturb our magic and our activities for the pure delight of doing so. This is particularly true as we endeavor to gain mastery over our mental body and dark thoughts, prejudices, negative thinking, and disruptive ideas seem to spring spontaneously into our minds. One can struggle with these, but in time one finds that this just feeds them energy. One learns to ignore them, give them no energy and to proceed onward in one's magic.

This is also, perhaps particularly, the case with ceremonial magic. The little demons and lower spirits will often chatter as one does one's ritual, saying it will fail, interfering with every thought, seizing upon any mispronunciation and ridiculing one. But again, the key is to move forward, correcting any mistakes immediately and without great ado, ignoring the chatter of the spirits that speak through one's mind, and completing one's magic. You can't really believe them, you can't really trust them, and really most of them just want to hear their own voices. They are enamored with their own chatter and do not wish it to cease.

And while some picture ceremonial magic in the same way that one views, say chemical formulas, where a misstep or a wrong portion of a chemical may lead to an explosion, or merely failure to produce the desired effect, in elven magic it is much more important to have the correct intention and proper ambiance than the exact right words or pronunciation. Most magic is like acting, in fact shamanism is the source of theatre, and if one flubs or forgets a line one merely improvises and covers it up, one goes on with the show. Elven magic is, in fact, mostly improvisational.

Guardian Angels

Many folks believe in guardian angels, they even believe that they have one especial angel assigned to watch over them all their lives. This is not quite the way elves view the world, although it is a sweet thought, if somewhat egocentric. There are higher spirits that look after us, particularly as we advance upon the path and thus draw their attention. However, it is rather silly to think that we each have one spirit that, like a valet, attends our every action. Rather, the spirits who look over us are in fact the greater powers that influence the region or domains we live within. Like children in a large family, we are one of many under their care. Also, like in a large family with many children, the elder children tend to look after the younger ones. So, too, do we in time become increasingly responsible for our kindred who are rising along our own path, and under our sway and persuasion.

Increasingly, we are expected to take care of our own s'elves, in fact, that is the point of our elven evolution that we become so powerful that we may venture into the realms of Faerie on our own. It is only when we are able to do so that we will be entrusted with, or have developed the power to create, our own realm, fulfill our particular vision, and spread our word, our magical spell, outward, affecting and influencing the world and attracting those who are akin to it. This is the Way, to become ever more powerful as spirits, ever more harmonious as souls, and thus to aid our others to do the same. We are linked inextricably together and can only rise as they rise.

It is important to remember the adage As Above/So Below or As Within/So About. We each are a microcosm of the Universe and contain the Universe within us. In mastering our own s'elves we gain power within the Universe and in time all we wish and desire comes to be.

There are, alas, many temptations upon the Way but besides the Guardians that have been sent to give us hints about the directions we may follow, there are also Sages from a variety of philosophies available to inspire us. The best way forward however is to ever remember that we are free to do whatever we wish but that all we do will come back to us multiplied, and that we are therefore responsible for all that we do. And to remember that we are connected to all things, which are in fact beings in the Universe, and that all we do to or for them, we are doing to and for our own s'elves. Our thoughts inform our actions, our actions shape our personality, and our personality becomes our destiny; we create our future in everything we do.

Bright Dawn of the Soulful Spirit

Most of us along the path encounter what is often called the Dark Night of the Soul, which we call the Dark Night of the Soulful Spirit. This occurs when one feels not only disconnected from everyone and everything in the Universe, thus the Dark Night of the Soul, but also when we feel at the same time that our magic is ineffectual, or that magic doesn't really work or exist at all, and we feel like giving up, thus the Dark Night of the Spirit. The soul is our link to others, the spirit our own sense of s'elfhood and empowerment.

All the world is a spell, or really a myriad of spells that have interwoven and created the world as it appears to us. Among these are dark spells designed to render us powerless, both as individuals and as a magical community. There are, alas, spirits who are undeveloped soulfully, who seek power for thems'elves at the expense of others and who only make alliances out of necessity for the sake of gaining personal power. These are ever uneasy alliances, for all their allies are soul-challenged as well and only hang together out of self-interest. These use magic designed to divide and conquer and promote prejudice and ethnic and social divisions in order to keep us from uniting and working together.

As elves, as evolved soulful spirits, it is our responsibility, as well as in our best interests, to see these dark spells for what they truly are, to master any prejudice we may have, to treat all beings with respect, and form alliances based, not only on mutual s'elf interest, but also on what is right and fair for all folk. It is important to understand that feelings of alienation from others, while often due to being rejected by those who don't except our magical elven natures, are ultimately the result of these dark magics, and we need to see through these spells and act in ways that supersede their power. In other words, we elves don't let other's disbelief in our magic or our elven natures affect our own belief and knowledge of our being nor do we let it affect the magic we use, in the form of courtesy and respect, in dealing with others.

The other aspect of these dark spells is a psychic assault upon our s'elf worth. The effects of these spells can be seen early on in the form of bullying, both physical or more often and more potentially damaging, emotional, mental and psychic harassment designed to make us feel less than, and powerless. The goal of this magic is not only an attempt to pressure us into conforming to their vision of society but also to convince us that we have no power or magic to combat them; that we might as well give up and do whatever they tell us to do. This is an attack on our spirit and part of the progress on the Elven Way is an attainment of a sense of unshakable s'elf worth and an unwavering knowledge that our magic, while not always immediately effective, will always be fulfilled in the long run. We are increasingly the masters of our own destiny.

When we come to the profound realization that depression, feelings of loneliness, a sense of powerlessness and alienation are all due to dark spells in the world, we experience the Bright Dawn of the Soulful Spirit and journey onward embracing the Elven Way with the knowledge that we are never truly alone, our elven kindred from various dimensions are ever supporting us. Our magic, hindered though it may be temporarily, is an expression of our true natures and we are inevitably headed toward the realization of our s'elves as powerful elven spirits.

The Dark Mirror

The other side of these dark magics, like a mirror, shows the reverse image of things. These dark spells seek to convince us that we can only succeed by conforming, by making alliances with other dark magicians and paying tribute to the more powerful dark ones above us, with an expectation that in time if we are cunning and clever enough, we may survive to replace them, surreptitiously undercutting those around us while pretending to be their friends.

At the same time, they tempt us to use our power (if they haven't convinced us we are powerless) for strictly selfish gains, to scorn others who have fallen into the trap of their spells as being weak, and thus easy and natural prey for them, rather than seeking the good of the whole. It is important to understand that while these dark magics may seem evil, they are in fact a function of the descent by spirit into the material world. They have arisen from the dog-eat-dog, one-up-manship, zero-sum game of survival of the fittest and simply lack the higher spiritual values that will aid all being in time to master the material world and re-ascend to our destined spiritual heights. Thus while we do not wish to fall for these dark spells, or participate in them, for they will limit our capacity to evolve to more powerful and inclusive dimensions of being, we also do not wish to get caught up in subjective feelings of hate toward those who espouse them, which would only hamper our progress. It is true that we sometimes must act very decisively to counteract their efforts, limit their magic, and keep them in proper boundaries. But for the most part this is best done from a transcendent point of view and is most effective when transpersonal in manifestation. These elves don't hate the people who project these dark magics, but we often find we despise their actions, although that, perhaps, is due to the limits of our own development.

It is important to consider that actions that are quite effective and even vital on one level of development become ineffectual and outmoded on the more subtle planes of being. However, we must also remember that we are here now because of who we are. Our own magic has brought us to this point, and it is our own magic that shall lead us further on the Way. Be not too quick to judge others, but ever ready to understand. That we seek personal power and success is only natural, however, we must understand that all others seek the same and that ultimately none of us can achieve what we truly wish without each other. That we seek the love, affection, recognition and acceptance of others is also natural, but we must do that without surrendering our own natures, our own conscience (conscious science, which is to say reasoning based on facts and awakened consciousness), or our own judgment concerning what is right and wrong. We are greatest when we are each powerful independent elfin magicians working together.

So, too, it often seems that we are prey to Nature. Utterly subjected to its whims and dictates. However, it is our destiny to Master Nature, both our own natures and greater Nature, but we do that by creating a harmonious relationship with Nature, not by controlling it at whim and certainly not by destroying it. We come to know its laws and use them to obtain what we will.

This soulful understanding of mutual power and harmonious interaction is a vital part of Elven Magic and a key to our progress through the dimensions. We are not destined to be puppets or to be puppet masters, but to be elves sharing and celebrating the Dance of Life, the Great Faerie Circle with all Beings. Our relationship with Nature and with Life is ultimately one of Love. We love Life and Nature, and Life and Nature will return that devotion as we become ever more in harmony with ours'elves, our magic, and with the principles that guide the Universe. The power we have over Nature, the power to influence and sway it, always begins first and foremost as we master our own inner being, our own natures.

Through the power, and under the guidance, of our conscience (again conscious reasoning), we gain mastery over our passions and direct their powers toward the realization of our vision. Our quest for personal power is balanced on our sense of fairness, thus we seek the empowerment of the better and higher natures of all beings. We increasingly come to understand that all we do affects us. All we do to uplift others, uplifts ours'elves as well, and all we do to improve ours'elves radiates in a positive way to others. There is no absolute separation, except in seeming. We are all interwoven threads of the Great Tapestry, the Magic Carpet of Life.

The strict isolation of our minds and consciousness is a temporary needful phenomenon as we develop these powers. In time our psychic abilities will increase multifold, but that will not happen for most of us until we have developed our mental powers to the point where we will not be overwhelmed and washed away by the psychic ocean. In other words, we will both be able to turn this energy on and off, as well as keep our own thoughts separate from those of others that we will hear internally. Those psychics who complain that their gift is a curse usually do so because they feel powerless to deal with the intrusive thoughts, visions and feelings of others. Thus one can see that the strict isolated consciousness that most folks experience is for their benefit and protection. As we develop as spirits, we will become strong enough to be more open as souls. Once again the evolution of the soul and spirit work in tandem. Therefore, in developing ours'elves it is usually best if we make effort on all levels. That is to say, we increase the power of our minds, the health and well being our bodies, our emotional maturity and relationships, and our spiritual understanding.

Nor need we be overly concerned about our place in the world. Our status in the world is not necessarily reflective of our level of development as elven spirits, nor vice versa. We should remember that this holds true of others and that it is unwise to judge others by their appearance, wealth or seeming success in society or lack thereof. At the same time, these aspects are not necessarily disconnected. Quite often our success in the world in some way reflects the functioning of our karma, or the spiritual challenges we have undertaken voluntarily to develop some aspect of our being, spirit, soul, or personality. For most elves, however, the question is quite simply one of: do you wish and are you capable of being our true friend or ally? If the answer to that is yes we will do all we can to aid you on your path. If the answer is no, we wish you blessings upon your way.

Our position in the world of Faerie is not dependent upon our success in the material world. It is utterly an effect of our spirit, our personal power, and our soulful development. The values of the material world are an illusion, a temporary manifestation that is only a dim reflection of the true world of energetic being. We increasingly come to understand as we move ever more deeply into Elfin that we are eternal beings living in Eternity.

> "THE TRUTH MAY BE PAINFUL, BUT THE FAILURE TO FACE THE TRUTH MAY KILL YOU."
> —OLD ELVEN WORDS TO LIVE WELL BY

We walk among them
But they do not see
That we are who
We wish to be
They think that we
Are crazily
A strange part of
Reality
And though from Faerie
We have come
To such truths
They're blind and numb
And though we stand before them
Clear
They say that we are never
Here
And though we do in passing smile
They do not see us all the while.

CHAPTER 5:
THE SANCTUARY

We, in many ways, begin our conscious elven life when we awaken to our elven fae natures. We progress upon it as we develop increasing control over our inner vehicles, that is as we do all within our power to improve our bodies, minds, feeling maturity, our soulful connections to others, and our personalities, will and spirit. When we have done that to a sufficient degree, and really it is in many ways a never ending quest, we are advanced to a level where we begin to understand the multiple nature of existence, to know that there are parallel worlds and dimensions and to understand that our choices create subtle shifts that lead us from one world to another. Naturally, as elves we seek to enter ever more deeply and profoundly into Faerie.

Having reached this third level of development, our contact with the Shining Ones increases, their interest and influence in our development becomes more powerful, and they begin to assess our being and the aspects that need to be developed to help us achieve our vision in harmony with the Great Vision and realization of our true elfin natures. We also become increasing attuned to the Star forces, the powers of Faerie, and our destiny. For those who are knowledgeable about Astrology, one's natal and progressed charts give one great insight into one's life task, capabilities in a particular lifetime, and the unfolding thereof. Most advanced elfin magicians have at least a cursory understanding of astrology and how to cast and interpret a simple natal and progressed chart.

At this point in our development, the Shining Ones send us lessons that are in accord with our own personal magical aspirations. These often unfold under the aspects of the rays of the elven star, the rays of manifestation. For instance, those who are developing first ray qualities of will and leadership, often seek to establish vortexes or covens, organize gatherings or other magical social events for the fae, and so forth. The fact that some of us, these elves included, are not very good at this is not entirely relevant except in so far as our resolve is tested. Those who are truly drawn to this task, which again, these elves don't seem to be, will continue on endeavoring to organize elfin groups or gatherings even when their earlier attempts end in failure. These failures are generally due to the fact that the individual simply does not have sufficient charisma as yet to attract enough elfin to their event, and the Shining Ones will send them lessons to aid them in developing their charismatic power. It should be noted, however, that there may also be other factors involved, material factors that interfere with the elf's efforts, but that, too, is really just another obstacle to eventually overcome.

For our own part, we realized, and this also is a possibility, that these elves simply were not suited for this particular effort, even though there were, and are, elven kindred out there requesting that we hold such gatherings. Alas, that is not our path in this lifetime, and we also, honestly don't have the prerequisite knowledge, or the personalities, to pull it together. One does not always have to accept fate, but sometimes it is easiest and wisest to do so, particularly when you do discover your path, which for us turned out to be occasionally holding classes on magic, and writing these books on elfin magic, culture, philosophy and spirituality. These demonstrate a third and fourth ray manifestation and, as it turned out, are better suited to our natures.

Know, however, that as one progresses on the third level of development, it is very rare that the elf doesn't find and work with at least one other fae. There are, of course, unusual cases where the elf is a strictly solitary practitioner, but as we say in most cases the elf finds another of hir kind to progress with, and in fact, this finding of the other or others, is in itself often an indication that one has begun to tread in the inner dimensions of Faerie.

However, in delving into these more ephemeral realms, the elf also has increasing contact, interaction, guidance and assistance from spirits that are, in essence, invisible in the material world in the same way that heat is invisible, the air is invisible, radio waves are invisible, etc. That is to say they are real spirits, real beings, real energy, but not necessarily easily observable to our mundane sight. Usually, one senses them more than sees them, feels their presence, their influence and perceives their guidance through one's intuition. Note that these beings do what they can to protect us from harm and steer us in the right direction. It is also at this stage that we tend to become increasingly aware of our feelings and experience them as being signs to guide us, and we come to the realization that ignoring our inner sense nearly always proves painful or disastrous. Karmically, we are on a very short leash. Not because we are evil, but because we are probationers in realms of great power where magic eventually becomes instantaneous.

It is these spirits also who maintain the portals that permit entrance into the Faerie dimensions. We connect to those dimensions not only by mastering our inner natures, clearing our karma, and making concerted progress on the path, but also by creating our own realms of Elfin, creating sanctuaries in our homes or elsewhere, which like temples, churches, mosques etc. that provide a spiritual place for their devotees to contact their god(s), create purified atmospheric realms that are similar in vibration to the faerie realms and are in fact Elfin/Faerie manifest. In these places we can most easily pass over into the transcendent dimensions of elven being. It is also these sanctuaries that help awaken other kindred who may visit the elf and sense instinctively that this is a place apart.

If the elves move, the vibration of these faerie realms move with them, much like Merlin's fabled apple orchard that went wherever he did; but at the same time, at least for a while, a vibrational residue of Faerie is left behind that has a subtle influence on those who come after. Although, in these elves personal experience the places we have lived in, and have established just such a sanctuary and then moved from, are usually either left empty for a long while, bulldozed down, or refurbished completely, and not because we have destroyed the place, we are in fact very conscientious tenants, but because from our point of view few normal people feel entirely comfortable with the power of Faerie so near. It arouses all their subconscious fear about the nether worlds and they instinctively desire to return things to normal.

Just as the normal folk are uncomfortable with too much magical faerie energy; it scares them and makes them feel uneasy, so, too, do elves progressing on the path often feel disconcerted about having to deal with mundane considerations over and over again when we are endeavoring to lead a magical spiritual life. However, it is important to understand and to remind ours'elves that we are here to master the material world. It is true, as we've said, that we do this first and foremost by mastering ours'elves, but this also includes mastering our reaction to the world and making our passage through the world as easy and effortlessly as possible. Obstacles are gifts from the Shining Ones to aid us in developing our magic. They are like weights we have to lift to grow stronger. And the more we embrace this *weight training*, the more we will find power and satisfaction in our encounters in the world. Also, for the most part these obstacles almost always develop along the lines of our personal weaknesses, which is why we perceive them as obstacles, and in confronting them and overcoming them, we become ever stronger as elfin spirits.

Attitude/spirit is most important here. The main thing is to transform our own inner feelings and reactions, in as much as possible learning to embrace these things, or increasing our ability to spot them ahead of time and to avoid them in some cases, but most of all mastering them within. Once we do that the world submits willingly to our guidance, instinctually recognizing a superior personality and yielding without conflict to our vision.

The Harmonies of Elfin

Some folks say that the world was created by the utterance by God of the Words of Magic and Power. We elves tend to think that it was created by the Fae singing a Song of Faerie Power. As we create our own ealds, our own sanctuaries, the Song of Faerie begins to fill them. If we listen closely to the silence, we can hear the Song calling us ever back to Faerie, which is to say to the realization of our true natures that inevitably make us ever more attuned to the Faerie dimensions. Ultimately, the Song of Faerie is the harmony created by our own beings.

Each of us has a true name. That true name is the vibrational sound that is issued by our true elfin s'elf, and is unique to us. As we become more and more powerful as elven spirits our song, vibration, grows stronger. As we become more and more mature as souls, we become ever more in harmony with the Great Song of Faerie. This song creates Faerie as it unfolds throughout the dimensions and our individual song is part of that Great Faerie Song.

Between lives elves progress through those dimensions, often viewed by some people as "heaven", called "devachan" by others, where we may rest, refresh and see the vision that will guide us through our next incarnation. Of course, we also pass through the demonic realms, where all our negative karma is tested and our weaknesses in terms of greed, lust, etc. come to the fore and thus denote the limitations and challenges placed upon us in our coming incarnation. In time, we come to understand and recognize that both these realms are essentially illusions, that the true nature of the Universe is infinite possibility and the greater mastery we have over our own natures, the more we can shape the world as we envision. But that is a very advanced realization, indeed, and for most of us experiencing the heavenly and the demonic they still seem to be a very real events. It is in truth but another dream, as all of life is a dream, and we destined in time to become master lucid dreamers.

It is however in these sanctuaries both in the material world, in our dreams, and in the period between incarnations that we come into contact more freely with other beings from all over the Universe and throughout the dimensions. Here only natural attraction and shared dharma draw spirits and souls together in a direct fashion for a vibrational exchange that proves invigorating for all parties. Often elfin spirits make alliances for future lives and it is at this point sometimes that certain spirits jump dimensions to be together, or migrate from one solar system to another for optimal realization. This is an infrequent occurrence; however, it does happen, which is why we sometimes find individuals from other worlds who are not yet quite used to working within a human body. This is often the case for various otherkin types. Note that for most energetic beings, this period between incarnations is essentially automatic. We are swept along, just as we are in dreams, making choices and selecting directions instinctually, a natural response to our essential nature.

Energy, Vibration and Spin

We, as beings, are essentially consciousness that attracts energy to it and shapes this energy by the vibration of our being, which is in many ways to say our spirit's inclination as well as illuminated development, and by our spin, which is one form of our personality, or in common parlance, the way we roll.

This energy of our being, depending on our level of development also indicates where we descend in order to manifest in the dimensions, which is to say how material or gross is our manifestation. This grossness, while seeming to have to do with solidity, really is an indication of how refined we are vibrationally, which is also to say how many limitations are upon us, and our magic. The more karma we have, the more the limitations that slow our magic and seemingly impede it; although ultimately we all get what we create in the course of evolution. This again is another reason for mastering our vehicles, for the more they are responsive to our vision, the more power we have, the less we intentionally and unintentionally create limiting karma for us, and the more rapidly do we receive response from our magic.

There are exceptions to this, of course. Some individuals intentionally take on limitations in order to strengthen parts of their character or being, just as individuals do weight training to make thems'elves stronger. And some individuals, out of the profound nature of their love, help bear the burden of karma for others in order to help them. Such s'elf sacrifice is a powerful thing and not to be underestimated, although it does temporarily seem to limit one.

Building Form

However, whatever level one manifests on it still, for the most part, has the aspect of seeming solidity or reality, just as a dream seems real when one is dreaming it. When we are in a particular dimension, bound by its limitations and laws, it seems real, that is to say it seems solid to us. However, this solidity can vary. In some realms we can walk though walls. The more subtle the dimension and the more powerfully evolved we are, the fewer limitations we encounter and the greater our power to do and achieve what we will. We increasingly become creators, builders of form. And that indeed is our destiny to create our own realms of being, our own eald/demesne.

Of course, we are not all the same, in fact, we are all unique and we tend to increasingly work and build in concert with each other. And we do this along the lines of the particularly rays of influence and sub-rays that are symbolized by the seven points of the Elven Star. Just as modern society has doctors, auto-mechanics, and other specialists, as well as having sub-specialties, just as there are surgeons, general practitioners, podiatrists, dentists, nurses and others in the medical field, so do we, as spirits tend to specialize using our particular talents to help create the realms of Faerie. All contribute to the manifestation of the Magic in actuality and the more harmonious we are, the more beautiful and powerful become the realms we create.

Understand that when we speak of building form we mean more than material seeming structure. We also mean building spirit, building soul-filled relationships, constructing positive thought forms and other aspects that make a realm whole. Some work in color, some weave feeling, some are masters of ideas, each interconnecting what they do best to create the marvelous realms of faerie being.

Again, this begins with the mastery of our own vehicles, calming our mind so it is a clear and effective tool of our will, maturing our souls so we interact harmoniously with all willing, reaching deeply into our feelings from which we receive information from all that is beyond us, and invigorating our spirits so we endure and become beacons of light and illumination for others.

These are, of course, interacting aspects of our being. A troubled mind arouses our feelings creating powerful emotions that then cloud the mind even further. A weak spirit inclines us to depressed thought forms and thus depressed feelings or in time to a total lack of feeling. An undeveloped soul makes it hard to relate to others, and have a compassionate understanding of their particular circumstances. A weak body becomes easily sick and sickness and pain cloud the mind and the emotions. Always, we strive to become whole as individual elves and to uplift all aspects of our being. But consciousness is supreme, for all else is a seeming and stems from it. Ever we seek to increase our conscious awareness.

Creation, Stability and Destruction

Some spiritual disciplines observe there are three basic forces in the Universe: the force of Creation, the force of Stability or Maintenance, and the force of Destruction or Dissolution. All new things come into being by virtue of the Creative energy. The energy of Stability serves to maintain this new thing, usually through increasing levels of bureaucracy, the establishment of rules and laws that eventually so stagnate the original energy that it dissolves under its own weight or yields to the destructive pressure of other more creative energies.

This is a natural process. All things that are created, and essentially all things beyond pure potentiality and undifferentiated energy and consciousness are created, tend to seek to return into their original state of pure energy. This is the tendency of Entropy. Our goal as elven magician enchanters is to create worlds and vehicles for manifestation that are essentially immortal and eternal. We do that by merging and combining these primary aspects of energy. That is to say, we create, and we maintain our creation by continually changing (dissolution) it, and improving it (re-creating). It is through continual evolution and therefore renewal that we remain at the height of our powers and keep the worlds, realms, we created alive and growing. Thus we maintain by means of change, flexibility and adaptability.

So, too, must we ever develop ours'elves as spirits. There is no perfection. There is only continuous perfecting. We become creative spirits continuously renewing all we encounter. Stability is found in motion.

It is true that these often function in cycles of activity and inactivity. Particularly in the more gross planes of manifestation where rest and sleep are vital to renewal and where we are often unconscious, asleep for much of the time. As we become more and more aware and conscious, we still sleep, or our body will rest, but we will obtain an awareness of deeper and deeper levels of consciousness. In time we come to understand that all is consciousness, and as we become ever more aware, we master death/sleep/unconsciousness.

Past Lives

Part of this growing awareness and expansion of consciousness includes looking inward and looking outward, looking forward and looking into the past. All we have ever been, all we have ever experienced lives within us. As we come to know ours'elves more and more, we get a sense of our past lives and all that we have been through to get to where we are. We can also use our feelings as antennae to connect to all that is beyond us. The Universe is a connected whole and all things are interconnected to each other. Through these connections we increasingly come to know more and more of the true nature of reality, as well as see the illusion ever more clearly, thus we know what is, what was, and how things are inclined to be.

Understand that in saying this, we know that we live in the Eternal Now. All possibilities exist simultaneously in this Now; but in looking into the future or the tendencies for ours'elves or others in the future, we are really getting a glimpse of our own or their direction or trajectory. Choices can be made that will lead one from this to that parallel world, putting energy into some possibilities over others. They all still exist simultaneously, but some, we might say, like light bulbs, are turned on while others are not. Our choices, in a sense, determine which light bulbs we illuminate to light our way and the way for our others; although, we prefer to think of them as Faerie Lights.

While we speak of choice, and there are many, in some senses once one has entered upon the Way there is only one real choice, that is to go on ever improving ones'elf and helping one's others, or to give up. But having made that choice there are myriads of sub-decisions that come into play.

Recapitulation

The Universe nearly endlessly repeats itself, replicates itself, as DNA and viruses demonstrate, and reinvents itself using the same forms in myriads of ways. Each atom essentially resembles a solar system, sleep is in many ways similar to death, and if Haeckel was correct Ontology recapitulates Phylogeny, which essential means our gestation in the womb recapitulates the progress of our evolutionary development as a species. From this, using the principle of As Above/So Below we can also deduce that our individual life recapitulates our evolutionary development as spirits, thus our many previous lives.

While we can wait until we have developed a very expanded consciousness to view what we have been in previous lives, we can also look at our past, particularly the period from our birth to our first Saturn return, which is at about 28 to 30 years of age, to understand in an encapsulated form our previous incarnations. All we have been is contained within us and can be seen reflected in our early years.

Sorcerers often use this technique of recapitulation not only to see their previous lives but to come to know thems'elves and their trajectory thoroughly so they can master their vehicles, that is their minds, feelings, and bodies, their souls and their spirits and in doing so enter that other, truer world, where soul and spirit are all that really matter. It is worth the time of nearly every elf to ponder one's early life and come to understand who one is by the changes one has experienced and particularly the choices one has deliberately made through one's life. Remember Magic is primarily Will Directed and Intentional Choice; although for some folks it is their unconscious inclinations that are making the choices for them. Their magic is primarily unconscious magic for they are, as yet, unable to accept the reality of magic consciously.

Of course, the soul also calls to us often in the form of experiences of Déjà Vu to remind us of events that have occurred in previous lives in an almost identical fashion, or individuals we have known with whom we instantly experience a sense of familiarity even though we've never met them previously in the present life.

Many elves experience a strong sense of lives spent in Elfin on other worlds, or of years spent training as an adept in the esoteric schools of ancient Egypt or some other ancient culture, which are in fact recapitulations of time spent training with the Shining Ones. These are all valid experiences, although one needs to be careful of simply resting on one's laurels, so to speak, and using past honors as an indication of present circumstances. The significance of the past is always in terms of a greater understanding that enables us to proceed more effectively upon the Way. We are not here to reclaim a Faerie that once was, but to participate in a Faerie that ever is.

At the same time, these experiences or psychic memories should not be discounted for they remind us of Elfin and the Elven Way and help us reconnect in a positive and ongoing fashion with our evolutionary directive, which is ever to become our true s'elves in harmony with other true s'elves.

The Seven Chakras

The seven rays of the elven star also relate to the seven chakras, although not in the same order and it should be pointed out that each chakra also has an aspect of each ray as the elf advances upon the path. The first chakra involves at its lowest form, survival; and it is connected to the first ray as a primary ray and the seven ray as a sub-ray. In its highest aspect it denotes the s'elf actualized individual, but in its lowest it indicates the drive by the individual organism to survive at any cost.

The second chakra brings a sense of abundance and pleasure in it highest form and has the sixth ray as a primary ray and the second ray as a sub-ray. In it's lowest form it seeks to move the survival urge from a day-to-day existence and continuous struggle to survive to one of at least temporary security. It seeks to move one a little back from the edge, or living on the edge, to a state of conditional safety. It often joins with others in order to do this, and will willingly submit itself to another's leadership to obtain this acceptance and security. This is the energy that leads to participation in cults.

The third chakra involves our sense of s'elf worth in the world and is connected to the seventh ray as a primary ray and the first as a sub-ray. It seeks to gain power in the world and ultimately leads on to s'elf mastery. It promotes will power. As it develops the individuals finds hir place in the world, so that sHe is uniquely hirs'elf and at complete peace and harmony with all others. It promotes fierce independence and incredible attractiveness at the same time. It is the energy that makes power an aphrodisiac.

The fourth chakra involves our ability to love and our connection to others. It has the second ray as a primary ray and the sixth ray as a sub-ray. It evolves from unthinking participation in a group to conscious realization and the acceptance of personal responsibility in terms of group association. One belongs to the group and still thinks for one's s'elf. It tends to function in consensus. It promotes compassion. It expands from personal love to more universal love while still promoting the personal. It ever increases our capacity for relationship and ever widens our acceptance of others while diminishing our prejudice and intolerance.

The fifth chakra involves our ability to communicate. It has the fifth ray as its primary ray and the third as its sub-ray. It seeks to know intuitively and begins with instincts. It develops science and technique and relies in time on knowledge but eventually it returns to direct intuitive knowing. Although this latter knowing is informed knowledge. It develops the educated guess.

The sixth chakra is the same as the fifth only it has the third ray as a primary ray and the fifth as a sub-ray. Its ultimate development involves pure consciousness and its science is the science of awareness. It is very much like the fifth chakra aspect, except it ever relies on one's inner knowing. It promotes s'elf knowledge and s'elf trust.

The seventh chakra is associated with the fourth ray. It is creative in nature. It is s'elf actualizing and it harmonizes all the other rays, thus all the other rays are its sub-rays. It is spontaneous, original, unique and self-contained. It radiates outward and creates other realms of being. It promotes synthesis, synergy, mutual acceptance, and integration of all one's abilities, vehicles and aspects of being.

The Elven Way is not only the Way of the elves but the Way to Elfin.
—*Ancient Elfin Knowledge*

"One can never understand someone they hate. A sympathetic compassion is the only tool for true insight into another being."
—*Elven WIsdom*

"WE ELVES SELDOM SPOIL OUR CHILDREN, BUT WE DO LET THEM RIPE PRETTY THOROUGHLY."

The Elven Way

Sheltered in a land of light
Where every tree does glow
Like a gem throughout the night
As tender love we know
Elfin dawn does softly greet
Us snuggled in our beds
As we pull the covers up
Above our nestled heads
Till someone rises
Sets the pot
To brewing on the stove
And soon aromas fragrant
Are drawing us in droves
And smiling now to greet the day
And the night to come
We set about our daring deeds
As softly we do hum
And valiantly the dishes do
Bravely every chore
Until we've done us every one
And there awaits no more
Save doing what we ever will
Our wishes to pursue
Creating magic wondrous
As dreams we make come true.

CHAPTER 6:
THE PROBATIONARY PERIOD

*I*n most spiritual and other disciplines, there is a probationary period. In the mundane world this is usually a set period of so many months or years, however, the true probationary period actually lasts as long or as short a time as the elven aspirant, that is the aspirant to the Elven Way and to the knowledge of elven magic, takes to come to the point where they have set thems'elves on the path and will never turn back. This is not so much a mental decision, although some will make it mentally, often again and again, but an inner forging of the elf, a determination of hir spirit and soul that may waver, may rest awhile, but never gives up. There is simply no going back. It is the point of no return for the elven spirit.

As we say, how long this takes cannot be known, at least by these elves, although the Shining Ones may have greater insight concerning this, for the period differs from elf to elf; but when it occurs the path opens before one and the Way goes ever on.

This should not be confused with the attainment of mastery over one's vehicles. That process almost always takes much longer; takes lifetime after lifetime of effort and is seemingly never-ending. However, each success serves to lead one to ever-greater success and personal power.

During this probationary period, one is often riddled with doubts. Is the magic real? Or is the elf just fooling hirs'elf with wishful thinking? Is it real for others, the elf wonders, but sHe is not advanced enough to manifest it hirs'elf? And will sHe ever be? Is the Elven Way a valid path, or should she retreat to more acceptable spiritual endeavors? All these doubts and more may plague hir until sHe does at last embrace the Way fully with all hir being. Remember these doubts are both tests of one's resolve, commitment and endurance, but also often originate from dark spells designed to draw one back into the world of conformity so one may be easily controlled. How is it that they are both a test and a dark spell? The Shining Ones turn everything to their advantage and the fulfillment of their great Vision.

One is also tested by personal loyalties. As one progress on the path one moves from *Blood is Thicker Than Water*, that is strict alliance to one's family, tribe, nation, ethnic group and so forth, to an increasing understanding that one's true family is not necessarily composed of those who share one's genetic heritage or societal upbringing. Symbolically, *blood is thicker than water* means that genetics are more powerful than feeling association. The truth is both of these elements can be powerful, and both can be faulted. Unfortunately not every parent loves or nurtures its child; and all too often true love turns into genuine hatred. We elves have our sayings also. One is: *Air is Lighter than Water or Blood*, which means that with enlightened understanding we can rise above all petty and limited associations. We also say: *Spirit Penetrates Everything*, which means that we can bring light and understanding to all individuals no matter how close or far they seem from us by using the power of our spirit.

The further we go on the path the more we tend toward extended families created upon spiritual values. Ours is an association as deep as the traditional family and as harmonious as the spiritual ashram. Our love becomes ever more accepting and Universal. All children become ours. And we nurture the souls and spirits of all we encounter, wherever possible, and whenever allowed. This does not mean that we eschew traditional families but rather that we have a more expansive understanding of what constitutes family. One gains a greater understanding of the interconnectedness of all life, an understanding that reaches beyond the appearance of death.

Meaning and Purpose

The Elven Way gives our lives meaning and purpose. We come to understand who we truly are, that is that we are spirits evolving and we establish a purpose in our lives, which generally might be expressed as aiding ours'elves and all others to fulfill ours'elves perfectly. That is to say, we become who are truly are, which is who we truly desire to be. Remember, we ever wish to be our own true s'elves as perfectly as possible, which means among other things to be happy and successful forever, to live Happily Ever After.

The nature of that s'elfhood, however, determines the course and nature of our purpose, which while always seeking to fulfill the great vision, will vary from individual to individual according to their nature and the tasks, and quests, they have undertaken. We could say the tasks assigned to us; for this is true as well. The Shining Ones do assign certain tasks to us, but it must be remembered that all participation in the Way is completely voluntary so it is just as accurate to speak of responsibilities we have assumed. While the Shining Ones are far advanced to us as soulful elven/fae spirits, they are not our Bosses, but our mentors and guides. Still, since we realize that they *are* so advanced it is only natural that we often defer to their greater knowledge and judgment and accept the hints and guidance they offer us. Besides, due to their superior development and personalities, we cannot help but be impressed and influenced by them. We desire to assist them for this gives us great happiness.

This Meaning and Purpose that we obtain upon the Way is no small thing. It is a true power and can be used to great effect. There are many in the world who feel that life is meaningless and without purpose and are almost entirely dispirited because of this. Yes, you are quite correct, this is due usually to another dark spell that has been cast upon them. And when one sees and realizes this, it helps one overcome these dark spells.

Some are so affected by this sense of meaninglessness that they commit suicide. Others are so affected by the sense of purposelessness that they idly squander their lives. What else is there for them to do? It is for this reason that we elves ever seek to empower our others. You may call it part of our job description. Although, for the most part, we don't think of this as a job, but as a bit of fun we are having in the Universe. What else is there to do but play with a purpose?

In many ways, it is the realization of this meaning and purpose that seals the deal, so to speak, and moves one from probationary or exploratory treading of the Way to a consistent, persistent and determined effort to evolve to greater realization of our entire being. When all else seems to fail, when we have been deserted by our seeming friends for treading the Way, when we have been scorned by the world for our belief in Faerie and Magic, and even more so for our efforts to live the Elven Way, it is this purpose and meaning that sustains us. And ultimately it is this purpose and meaning that empowers us, rewards us, and gives us an unerring sense of direction.

Of course, as we've said Faerie is accessed primarily within us, although it also exists without us. Ponder that a moment. Thus the unerring sense of direction we develop through the attainment of purpose and meaning, acts first in terms of instinctual and intuitive guidance from within us. However, this inner understanding nearly always leads us to the right actions, or in some cases non-actions, in the outer world, leading us to those individuals and events that will further us on the way, as well as those we will further on their way.

It is true that this sense often takes a bit of honing. We must learn to trust its guidance and while we need to analyze our actions in keeping with our understanding of the Elven Way, we need also come to trust that these deep inner feelings are an accurate guide for us, despite what our emotions may urge us to do, or what our mind or the minds of others may otherwise suggest to us. This takes time and experience, but if one always does one's best, the best eventually comes.

Getting Ahead of Ones'elf

It is commonly the case that those who are still functioning on a probationary level, that is to say those who haven't entirely devoted thems'elves to the Way and who often are just exploring Faerie temporarily as a sort of passing fad, will frequently declare thems'elves to be far more advanced than they are currently manifesting or have achieved through the lifetimes. But this can be misleading for they may still be recapitulating earlier lifetimes and at the end of that recapitulation be in or near the place they currently claim.

There is a temptation for those who are slightly more advanced to want to set these neophytes straight, that is burst their bubble, prick their inflated ego, and otherwise put them in their place relative to their own more advanced position. These elves understand and sympathize with both these positions, since we've also experienced them ours'elves. However, we have come to the realization and the position that those elves who are youthful in spiritual development, or even more often young in age and still recapitulating previous lifetimes of development, are merely expressing their aspirations. If they brag to us that they are a king or queen, prince/princess or other nobility or one of the Shining Ones, but display not the least indication that they have actually obtained such lofty positions, we don't disparage them, nor deny their assertions. Rather we accept what they tell us as their true aspiration. What they are saying is that they are destined to be an elf king/queen, or that is their desire at this point and we see it as our duty to help them achieve this lofty goal. It benefits all of us if they are greater and more advanced upon the path than they currently are. We know that psychologically they are really telling us both that they hunger for recognition to be someone great, but they are also saying they wish to do great things, and is exactly what we wish for them as well.

Those young elfin also tend to relate to us amazing tales of past lives and adventures on the astral planes, etc. and again we don't reject these claims. They are a shamanic reality at the very least, even if they have no other validity. These claims are also a psychological revelation. Some may say that they are just fantasizing, and this may be true, but fantasy and imagination are keys to magic, as well as often offering insights into faerie culture and enchantment; and we tend to encourage this activity rather than discourage it. In time they will learn to link their fantasies to reality, transforming real events in the world though a shift in their perceptual awareness and understanding and see them as the magical events they truly are, and this will denote a true advance for them. Discouraging them would only hinder this development. Our goal always is to nurture them toward the realization of their true s'elf, however they may envision that for themselves. And if a bit of fantasy helps them to come a bit deeper into Faerie, well, that is its purpose after all. We ever remind ours'elves that fantasy is merely the wondrous velvet that Faerie wears, beneath that is the naked and glorious reality of Faerie life.

Vows of Poverty

Many spiritual paths take a vow of poverty, and while the Elven Way is similar in many senses to other spiritual or religious orders, we have no such vow, although one might think otherwise if one viewed the currently rather limited financial circumstances of most modern elves. On the contrary, we elves feel an obligation to improve ours'elves financially, just as we feel we have an obligation to improve our health, strength, education and so forth.

Simultaneously, even though we feel this necessity to succeed in the world, our devotion to the Elven Way is an even greater impulse and when these two forces come into conflict we will willingly sacrifice financial success and social acceptance for success upon our spiritual path. It is not due to a vow of poverty but a devotion to the Way, which resembles in many ways the marriage vow: *to love, honor and cherish, for richer or poorer, in sickness and in health, now and forever more.* We do not abandon our own, or the Way, due to an alteration in circumstance nor do we unite with others because of what they possess or their social standing. We are ever loyal and our relationships are based upon the magic and the enchantment between us.

It is true that in living the Elven Way we often come into contact and interact with those individuals treading the path to whom we may not normally be attracted; but as we develop as elven soulful spirits we increasingly see the beauty in all individuals and our ability to harmonize with others continually increases. However, that does not mean we thus have an obligation to be involved with everyone who comes along. Some are simply not meant for us, although we do our best to help them on their way. We do not ignore our personal and instinctual attractions; rather we expand their parameters.

It is also true that most elf folk endure a prejudice from the normal folk due to the fact that they instinctually realize that we are different from them, even when we do all we can to fit in; an effort that most elfin give up in time realizing it is, in fact, a near hopeless endeavor. This social prejudice is also a bar to our pecuniary endeavors. However, in time we also come to realize that while many hold a prejudice against us for being, as they would put it, weird, that they instinctually prefer us to be our own true s'elves rather than pretend to be other than we are, which always makes people uncomfortable. In fact, it is in part this constant pretending, this need to put on a front that has normal folk ever uncertain about each other, so you often hear them saying, "Well, you just never can tell about someone, can you?" It is also the acceptance of ours'elves and the Way that frees our energy to pursue success in the world without constantly wasting energy putting on a false image for social acceptance. For the elves, our persona, our personalities, and our true s'elves are very similar. What you see is what you get for the most part, although, there is always something more, deeper and richer, as you get to know us. We have hidden depths.

This difference in the elven nature, that the normal folk so often refer to as being weird, is due in part to the fact that we come from a culture and a spiritual heritage that values cooperation over competition, and happiness over material success and possessions. Thus the modern world and its emphasis on making money is in many ways a mystery to the elven spirit. These are never our primary goals as they are for so many folk.

Therefore, while we don't take a vow of poverty, in fact quite the opposite, we vow to do all we can to succeed in order to help our people; poverty is often the lot of the elf in the world. We will, however, in time, lifetimes perhaps, get better at negotiating the world and becoming financially independent. Every elf instinctually seeks financial independence. But again we will not compromise our spiritual path in order to do so, for if we did that we would sink back into the normal world and eventually become like those who are even now in danger of losing their souls, in addition to dulling their spirits by continually denying their true s'elves because of a desperate need to fit in. This is not our way. As our dear elf brother Jesus asked, what profits an elf if sHe gains the world but loses hir soul and spirit?

And elves, by and large, ever seek to gain money, as well as nearly everything else, by means of magic. This may seem strange to some, although much of the world actually engages in this activity as they do various magics to win the lottery, or get that job they want or whatever, and in that way we are no different, except that money and financial independence is ever a means to an end, not the end in itself, and for us it is just another exercise in magic. We're always practicing, endeavoring to refine and increase our abilities.

The elf who has risen in the world naturally feels an obligation to assist hir others as best sHe may. Being a free spirit, it is up to the elf to decide the extent of the obligation and how it can best be fulfilled. It is not our way to tell others what they should do, although if we can provide a helpful hint we will do so.

Transpersonality

Besides gaining mastery over our passions, our tendencies toward anger and so forth, we develop a state of inner calm upon the path that leads us to be unmoved by the passions of others. That does not mean we don't acknowledge those passions, or are insensitive to others feelings but that we increasingly develop a capacity to be personally unaffected by accusations and anger that others may direct toward us.

There are some who believe we elves are an unfeeling folk, or without passion, (rather like Vulcans our imaginal kindred in Star Trek) but as we've said previously this is not the case. Rather we become increasingly transpersonal in our dealings concerning things that to us seem to be on the order of soap opera dramatics. We are as unmoved by these inflated and dramatized passions as we are by the barking of dogs, which does not mean we are not aware that dogs sometimes bite, but we don't tend to bark back and aggravate them further as we've seen many folk do, nor do we take their barking as a personal affront or insult.

Nor are we elves prone to hatred, which is to say we don't tend to hate people, although we do often hate the incredibly ignorant and intentionally wicked things they do. We ever try to keep in our hearts and minds the reality that all beings are striving toward success as spirits and to nurture the positives aspects of their being. It is true that sometimes there is nothing we can do for certain spirits at this stage in their progress and we have, and feel, no obligation to be involved in their dramas.

The best thing we can do for most people is allow them to make their own mistakes, give them no energy at all, and be on our own Way furthering the good and bringing the Radiance of Faerie into the world in our own fashion. It is important to remember that each individual has a right to determine their own fate/karma and they are doing so with every action that they take. If they ever come to the place where they truly wish our help, they will most certainly ask for it. It does no harm usually to offer assistance, but remember most folks don't really want your advice and are unlikely, which is to say not ready, to follow it anyway.

And keep in mind that counter to any appearances, no one gets away with anything in the long run. You may find yours'elf in a situation where you feel obligated to take action to curb or combat evil and if that is the case you have our heartfelt wishes for your success. Believe us, we support you in your efforts. But quite often individuals on a probationary level get involved in transitory conflicts of a personal nature that are really none of their business and their life would be much better, and things would go easier for them, if they avoided these entanglements. Still, as a free elven spirit it is always up to you to decide the level and amount of your involvement, and if you get it wrong from time to time, we have faith that you will learn and will do better in the future. We did and you are surely smarter and wiser than we were. You are after all most likely the next generation, the advanced model, the new and improved elf and quite possibly our own s'elves reborn.

It is important to understand that in stepping upon the path of elven magic that we are evoking the Shining Ones and the powers of Faerie to aid us to fulfill ours'elves as individual spirits and they will send us those things, people, experiences and challenges that we need to get to where we wish and where we need, by virtue of our own inner being, to be. We can, although it is truly a waste of energy and wiser not to, complain about our fate. This is the path we are on, this is where we are at the moment and it is from here that we must proceed. If sometimes circumstances seem overwhelming this is just a reminder that our magic is not as yet as powerful as it should and will be.

Suffering

There are some who think that suffering is necessary to develop spiritually and that, in fact, the path is all about suffering. However, we elves see our path as doing all we can to alleviate suffering in the world, and we are surely intent on avoiding it ours'elves as much as we are able to do so. We are not here to suffer; we are here to overcome suffering. In as much as it is in our power we are here to remove the causes of suffering from the world.

On the other hand, magic requires energy and effort and although as we master our art we become ever more proficient at it and thus it may seem effortless, a lot of time and energy goes into it becoming that way. And, yes, sometimes we do suffer in the world, but that is not what the Shining Ones wish for us, it is not our destiny, although it is sometimes our fate. Suffering tells us we are not as powerful and strong as magician enchanters as we need to be, and we endeavor to understand it that way, and to use it as a basis of honing our spirits and deepening our souls. Thus, like the Shining Ones, we turn all things, including obstructions to our ultimate advantage.

Our goal, and in many ways our shamanic method we remind you, is ecstatic union with the Divine Magic of Elfin. This state of ecstasy masters all lower experiences, overcomes all pain and suffering and eventuates in the healing of our minds, souls, bodies and spirits.

It is important to understand, however, that as you gradually or even suddenly move from the probationary state of your quest, you will be rising higher and higher, becoming more and more evolved in contrast to the mass of humanity around you. It is inevitable that many of the individuals you encounter will disappoint you, fail to live up to your expectations (if you are so foolish as to have them), and they may end up acting in a selfish fashion which may seem like betrayal to you. What do you expect? They are not yet evolved to your level and such inferior modes of acting simply reflect their current level of development and karma. We urge you to have patience, compassion and a cautious understanding of the shortcomings of others. Treat them as equals, for this encourages and empowers them; never put on airs for that just reflects one's own shortcomings; but also don't expect them to be more than they are at the moment. Increasingly as you tread the path, you will become both more harmonious as a spirit and more independent, that is less emotionally and financially dependent, upon others. True love only lasts between two or more strong and equal spirits.

And remember, no matter how far along the path you are, how advanced you are compared to others, you still have your own inner challenges to overcome and master. We are none of us perfect, but all seeking perfection. Particularly in this mundane world this serves us well, for you may have noticed that most people hate those who seem perfect. If we get too far beyond those we seek to assist, we have no way to connect to them. Be your own true s'elf and that will be both perfect and imperfect enough to delight the hearts of everyone who has a soul.

Poetic Justice

Some religious and spiritual philosophies warn their devotees against pursuing revenge and we elves both agree and disagree with this philosophy. It is true that hate entangles us subjectively with the hated and that is not our desire; rather we wish to move forward in a positive fashion and ever strive to do so. It is also true that everyone eventually receives their just due, the consequences of their actions, and that is an

The Elven Way

inescapable law of the Universe. However, we elves don't simply let everything pass without response, excepting that God or Goddess or the Shining Ones will take care of it for us. We also have a duty to curb evil and sometimes find ours'elves in a position where we may be called upon to punish those who have transgressed against us, or ours or the innocent.

This action, however, should not be personal in nature. It is not about redressing a personal insult or wrong, but about establishing order in our realm. Remember, you are an elven magician/enchanter and are the center of your own magical circle, your eald, your spiritual realm and dimension. You have an obligation to keep this realm in working order and to correct the spirits that transgress, not only for the benefit of the realm but for their own spiritual development as well. This is not a matter of revenge, although at times it may be important to take action in secret, particularly in cases where the spirit involved is more powerful in the world or likely to retaliate, for we are acting as, and with the authority of, the Shining Ones. This action thus often needs to seem to come from the invisible dimensions. Again, this is not personal in nature, although we may take personal delight in their comeuppance, and we are not interested in prolonging or starting a feud, rather we seek to end all feuds. It just happens that punishment or the threat of punishment, for those who are as yet not very evolved, sometimes serves as an effective deterrent to further misdeeds.

At the same time it should be said that most elves, like most spirits in fact, enjoy seeing someone get their just due, delight in poetic justice particularly where the individual has unwittingly brought about hir own doom through the consequences of hir misdeeds. Some may wish to stand back and let the Universe take care of all such actions, and in time it surely will. And it is our observation that those elves who refuse to respond to any wrong, always trusting that the Universe will act in their stead, although these are few, are right to do so. Their path and their future is not one of the administering of justice and fairness. But many of us are being prepared for a future among the Shining Ones where we will be Lords of Karma or other such disciplinarians, kings or queens of our own ealds, adjusting circumstances so that each spirit will get those challenges and obstructions, and some times timely warnings, that will guide them to their own fulfillment.

The important thing to remember again is that this is not personal, but transpersonal. This is not a conflict between two spirits, or between egos, as it may seem, for our ultimate goal is ever harmony and union. It is rather the natural adjustment to create a greater order in our realm and our actions should never be personally offense. We are not trying to prove we are better than they are, or better than they have accused us of being, but we are rather truly endeavoring to rise above the situation and do what is in fact best for all concerned.

What is most important, for you and them and all others, is that you do what is fair. Our actions need to reflect an attempt to bring the world into balance. Magic always returns to us and all we do shapes our future. Remember this always.

The Transference of Power

One can always strive alone, but most often our success and our increasing power depends upon the invocation of the powers of those allies who are our mentors and benefactors. There are certain things that we need in order to evolve that can best and most easily be learned by personal contact and interaction. We must see the magic in action. We need to absorb, in the form of osmosis, the higher vibrations that will increase our personal frequency, quicken our evolution, awaken our consciousness and increase our capacity for magic. In yogic circles, this is seen as the blessing and grace of one's guru. Unlike some traditions where it is often said that one cannot progress without this personal contact, we elves know that we can progress on our own with devoted and sustained effort.

However, this contact makes it so much easier. It helps one make a quantum leap from one level of development to a higher one. Thus we elves ever seek those individuals, those great spirits, from whom we can learn, and whose example is ever an inspiration to us.

And naturally, as the probationary aspirant makes alliances, increases in power and rises upon the path, the elf's capacity for more power increases. Soon the probationary stage of one's experience on the Way falls behind one, although in most cases one is too busy pursuing the Elven Way to take notice. Are you a probationer? It is for you to say. It is ever your own decision to devotee yours'elf or not that is the true answer to this question. Naturally, we, and all elven kin, delight in those who join us in exploring and sharing the inner reaches, dimensions and realms of Faerie.

Evoke Often

As our brother Aleister advised us, *Evoke Often*. Like all things, practice, plus a devoted effort to improve what one does, makes perfect. The more we do our magic with a scientist's eye to what works, that is what produces a result, and what doesn't work, thus continually refining it and adapting it to changing circumstances, the better we get at it. The constant of elven magic is that it is ever changing and adapting to different circumstances. Since this magic emanates from our own s'elves, it is ever we who become increasingly adaptable. We, and the magic, are one.

We might imagine that there is within us a muscle, a psychic muscle that we develop by exercising it. Creating grand ceremonies and calling spirits within a circle, while interesting, valuable, and a delight, tends to be a rare thing, requiring a great deal of time and effort, thus tending to be infrequent. Rather, integrate your elfin magic in your day to day life, casting your spells unseen even among the mass in public, making your every act and effort an act of elfin magic. Do this and Faerie will spring up all around you. The Song of Faerie will echo in silence to the inner ears of those you pass and magic will become your life and Elfin the place of your abode. This is not to say that you shouldn't, when moved to do so, create more elaborate rituals, rather that you will get less practice if you confine your magic only to special occasions.

We Are Magic

We do elven magic, yes, but increasingly we find that we are the magic, that the magic flows from our inner being and that all that we do therefore is magical. Magic for the elves is not a task that we do, like washing the dishes, although we do make washing the dishes a magical act, but an effect of our being. As this becomes increasingly so, we depart from the uncertain realms of indecision and move ever more deeply on the Way. We are no longer trying out being elven, we are elves and increasingly all we do is elven.

It is the same with love, which in the elven mind is essentially the same as magic. Most elves are ever seeking a loving connection in the world, but we do this by being loving. We know that what we do creates what we are and that our karma, fate and destiny follow therefrom.

In doing this, the elf penetrates the Mist that surrounds Faerie and the radiance of a bright Elfin day is seen beyond. We enter Faerie by becoming our own true s'elves. We are the light that the moths of Faerie are drawn toward; we become the radiance that is reflected and Faerie reciprocates.

We become thus a light unto others who seek, and though this is often a gentle light, a subtle light that it takes true sight to see, it none-the-less affects all we encounter, although few are advanced enough to realize this. And for our own part, we are ever focused on our own inner light that shines from the heart of Faerie. The further training and powers we need come to us naturally, often in the form of, or the company of, synchronicities. We see into the parallel dimensions, and the spirits that dwell there appear to us almost as if they were ghosts, although they are not. They are just more ephemeral in substance than we. We gain power in association to the elementals who willingly assist us as they come to recognize our authority. We interact with the devanic, angelic, faery folk of various realms and make allies among them. And we thus live in vaster world of conscious realization and awareness.

Four things become important in expressing this magical authority:

1. We need to become certain of our ours'elves and our magic. We need to set aside doubt and act with confidence. We need to proceed fearlessly forward, sure in our path and the radiance of the powers we evoke.
2. While these powers can be used to fulfill personal desires, those desires should never be obstructive or contrary to the flow of enlightened evolution. By placing ours'elves in harmony with the Universe and its Laws, which is to say its Nature, and by keeping the Vision and the principles of the Elven Way ever in mind, we are protected from any enduring harm and free from accumulating negative, thus obstructive, karma. The highest use of these powers always combines the personal and the Universal.
3. Inner calm and serenity are vital. In dealing with the more ephemeral spirits, one is dealing with beings who are exceptionally sensitive, particularly to feelings and emotions. Agitation is in most cases counterproductive, although intense and passionate ecstatic emotion can be very effective, but even these are best if used from a base of serene and measured mastery. In many ways, dealing with these beings is like being a beekeeper. You really don't want to agitate the bees. Perhaps, in part, this is the reason that the ancient elven

bloodline of the Merovingians had the beehive as its symbol.
4. Thus it is important to understand the forces that one is dealing with. Are you interacting with elementals, spirits, the Shining Ones? Just as one must be careful in putting in electrical wiring in a house, or sailing on the ocean, one needs to understand their environment, the elementals involved and how to safely interact with them. Caution and thoroughness are therefore advised.

If one reaches this point then one is ready and most definitely begins to enter the inner dimensions of Faerie and Elfin Magic. The mists clear, the Way opens, and one progresses ever onward, lifetime after lifetime becoming ever more and greater in harmony with the Shining Ones, with Faerie and all our kindred who also so strive. We are glad you are here. We've been awaiting you. There is much to do and other kindred yet awakening who are just beginning to tread the Way who need our help and guidance.

It is time now to go further, deeper into Elfin. The Way opens before us and we need only step forward.

THEY SAY THE FIRST STEP IS HARDEST
AND SURELY THIS MAY BE
FOR GETTING STARTED TAKES A BIT
OF DOING, DON'T YOU SEE?
AND THOUGH WE SOMETIMES STUMBLE
AND SOMETIMES WE DO FALL
AND SIT UPON OUR BACKSIDES
AND WONDER IF THE CALL
WAS TRULY WHAT WE THOUGHT IT
OR WAS IT FANTASY

The Elven Way

MERELY WISHFUL HOPING
FOR HUNGERED ECSTASY
BUT THEN WE DO REMEMBER
THAT BEFORE WE TOOK THAT STEP
THE WORLD DID SEEM A VACUUM
THAT MEANINGLESS HAS KEPT
TO HOLD US EVER OCCUPIED
WITH THIS AND THAT AND T'OTHER
LIKE TOYS TO KEEP US BUSY
AS WE HUNG ABOUT OUR MOTHER.
THEN WE EMBRACE THE JOY WE FELT
WHEN FIRST WE TREAD THE WAY
AND SHARE THE WONDER OF THIS TIME
ON EACH AND EVERY DAY
FOR MEANING DOES TRUMP EMPTINESS
EACH AND EVERY TIME
AS WE DO TAKE ANOTHER STEP
TOWARD THE LIFE SUBLIME.

> WE ELVES LOVE PRESENTS, BUT THE PRESENCE
> WE LOVE THE MOST IS YOURS."
> —ELVEN TRUTH

CHAPTER 7:
REALMS AND DIMENSIONS

*T*he Awakened Elf who has embraced the path fully differs from those who still waver in their devotion, who are in effect probationers (although always of their own choosing, for our choice is ever to embrace them and draw them fully into our frasority). The Awakened One has developed power and has a certain control over hir life due in great part to hir orientation of that life in accordance with the Laws of Nature and the Universe, to what may be called Occult Laws, the inner and more subtle laws that govern life and evolution. This individual has taken control over hir life, strives to develop hir character as a soulful spirit, continues to educate and train hir powers, skills and abilities, particularly hir magical powers, and has demonstrated that sHe is devoted to hir people and the furtherance of the Way, the evolution of life, and the enlightenment of all beings.

SHe has thus demonstrated hir fitness for further occult/magical/esoteric training that will enable hir to safely use power and occult forces on the inner planes, that is to say the more etheric planes of being, the mental, astral and spiritual planes and use these powers to affect the material world of *man* or manifestation.

As the I Ching informs us (see our book the *Elven Book of Changes*) there are two primary ways one can proceed with this power. The first is to use it in the world by awakening other elves, involving ones'elf in establishing a vortex, coven, elf group/family, teaching in the world or getting involved in social and/or political issues such as saving the trees, whales, equal rights etc. or endeavoring to change the political atmosphere of a country toward a more tolerant, compassion and caring social process. Many elves very eagerly pursue this course and in fact, it is the path that these elves have, for the most part, followed. This path concerns using power in the material world, although it should be said that this is a primary path and even those who tread it, or the alternative, often find that they are developing thems'elves in regard to the other path as well. You may think of it as having a major and a minor course of study as is usually the case in undergraduate school.

The other course is more meditative in nature. One attunes ones'elf to the forces of Nature and begins to direct them, or one attunes to the more subtle forces of the Universe and interacts more directly with the Shining Ones and prepares to take one's place among those who direct the more subtle forces of the Universe on the various planes of being and the parallel realms and dimensions. This way also involves one in interacting with the subtle energies of the Earth, the ley lines, and other currents of power; and Feng Shui is often a course of study when one pursues this way.

As we say this second path is more meditative in nature and involves the use of creative visualization, imaginal practice and the delving into the nether realms of shamanic being. One is less concerned here with the current political climate and the nature of the world and more concerned with the etheric climate of spirit and soul. In both cases, but particularly in the case of this second one, the development of the individual character is of vital importance for from this development all else stems.

Again, it is seldom that one functions in just one of these realms, in fact, they very much depend upon each other, particularly the first on the second. And in the second one the first mode is reflected by action in a greater and more encompassing world. But it is still a world none-the-less and while the spirits one is involved with there are not human, or no longer human, or perhaps greater than human, they are still conscious beings with which one interacts. Those that primarily follow the first path, however, that is acting with others on the material plane are destined to become Masters who elevate the *human race* and bring enlightenment to *man* (we use this term here generically to indicate all sentient manifested earth beings, which is to say those who have reached the stage where personal choice begins to determine their fate and karma).

These Masters, or teachers, function specifically to add the development of others. Theirs is a particularly soulful, which is to say social or connective, path and they endeavor always to spot those who are ready for advanced training and to offer these those events and tests that will hone their spirit, enlighten their minds, and uplift their souls. As such they take their place within the hierarchy of the Shining Ones. By this we mean that their teachings, or classes, are held on various levels: from those just awakening on the material plane to advanced classes for higher adepts. We might see this in the same sense that there is elementary school, high school, college, graduate study on the masters level, and doctoral studies, and so forth.

These Masters also function in various aspects. Just as we have professors of history, philosophy, etc. there are Masters of each and all of the Seven Rays of manifestation. There are also Masters who deal with individual students and those who deal with the race overall or any of the various sub-races. Here we are referring to spiritual races, rather than race as a physical aspect of being as it is currently viewed, that is Oriental, Caucasian, etc. or as a cultural and ethnic group as it was viewed in the past, the French race, Teutonic race, and so on.

Those Masters of the inner path, however, are not directly or deliberately teachers, although one may surely learn from them if one has the Sight. These individuals tend to develop weather-working skills and in time oversee the development of flora and fauna on a planet to make it habitable to life, particularly advancing sentient life forms. The image of faeries taking care of the trees and flowers has a practical manifestation in these advanced elfin beings. These adepts also are in charge of creating the atmospheric conditions: physical, mental, spiritual and soulful that are conducive to advancing evolution.

These all take place under the guidance of the specific Shining One whose Vision, in harmony with the Great Vision, is being brought to life. All those who assist this great elven being will in time create their own worlds in a similar way. Of course, here we are speaking of very advanced work for which we are but elementary students at this point. However, on whatever level we currently are, we each study with and assist a particular Master in order to obtain Mastery in the same field.

It is most likely and important to understand that we were once cells in the body of this being. These cells have become enlightened, that is conscious, and in a sense we are still cells in this being's body, only ever more independent, conscious and aware and someday as we advance into the creation of our own faerie realm the cells that are currently composing our bodies will be assisting us as independent beings in essentially the same way, developing their own being toward greater realization and mastery.

It is of note that most of what this Shining One does is carried out by way of inspiration and spiritual upliftment. We, as experts in our fields of endeavor, are left to our own creative impulse to carry out the Vision as we are best able to do under this being's guidance. Once again, we are not slaves to this being, or mindless robots, but advancing adepts who use our own powers toward the fulfillment of the vision. We may consider this in terms of individuals working to create a movie. The costume designers, the set designers, the actors, etc. each contribute their own creative expertise to the project giving life to the director's vision. It is the harmonious blending of these talents that leads to the fulfillment of that vision.

Like making a movie, or creating a painting or a piece of art, the process sometimes seems chaotic. It is important not to judge the piece until it is finished and can be seen in its entirety. So, too, the various conflicts that occur within and between countries, ethnic groups, and civilizations are often the working out of the Plan, the blending of primary colors to create something great. In the lower orders this often means war and conflict; however, the more one advances as an adept the greater one's ability to interact harmoniously with others and the easier the process becomes. None-the-less, we are often dealing with primal and primitive forces, for that is what we are here to do and the process of uplifting them often involves suffering on their part, but really that is their choice, an effect of their free will with which we have no right to interfere.

And while the Shining One who guides our evolution and the fulfillment of hir Vision in material reality does so according to hir own insight, sHe still interacts with other Shining Ones so that hir vision and theirs interact harmoniously. Also, of course, while hirs is the primary vision, sHe has available to hir the expertise of other Shining Ones who have gone before hir or who have a particular knowledge that would be of value in hir creation. As ever, on nearly every level, we elves, like all artists, are inspired by each other, formulating new creations based on the ideas and inspirations that come to us from viewing another's creations.

Of course, above the specific Shining One who guides the fulfillment of the Vision on any particular solar system and thus the development of the various Root Races that lead to the illumination of the spirits growing therein, there are also Shining Ones who supervise the evolution of galaxies, and galactic systems and so forth. In a certain sense these form a sort of hierarchy, but in another sense each finds and follows the path with which they are comfortable, that they are drawn toward, and which fulfills their own spirit, just as some individuals enjoy teaching elementary school, some high school, some college, and some function as administrators of each of these. Each spirit follows hir own inner directive. It is true that sometimes, perhaps often the great Shining Ones above us know us better than we know ours'elves, see potentials in us that we as yet do not see, and thus offer us opportunities and challenges to awaken these aspects of our spirit. But ultimately it is always free choice that calls our destiny to us and creates our karma.

You can see those who are developing into guides for solar activity in the lives of those elves who nurture the spirit and souls of other elves in this lifetime, as well as in those who by their nature gather others and organize them toward various artistic or familial projects. You may note that there are others who aspire toward these things, such as holding elf gatherings and so forth who as yet do not have the power needed to fulfill their vision entirely. They may not as yet know what to do, or in doing it receive little or no response. However, if they continue on this path they are certain to receive assistance from the Shining Ones and will develop the skills of enchantment, the charisma and/or administration needed as well as the knowledge to make their efforts a success. They need not despair. Nothing we do is lost. All effort builds, accumulates and strengthens the muscles of our spirit and shapes our future.

Generally speaking one falls under the guidance of those who one experiences as being charismatic and inspiring. Thus the connection to those Shining Ones is quite natural, rather than arbitrary as it is often the case in one's work in the world or in the social political sphere. We are naturally drawn toward those who will guide us, just as those we are to guide will naturally find their way to us. Thus it is ultimately a hopeless thing to try to woo favor from others, or to cling to those who do not feel inclined toward us. They are not really meant for us and it is a waste of our time in the long run to put more energy toward the relationship than the situation calls for. This is often seen in romantic relationships where a person is in love with someone who has no interest in them. A certain dignified reserve is advised in such circumstances. It should also be noted that those who are meant for us, who will become our close allies or assistants will often, but not always, manifest in our lives in a romantic fashion, for our relationship to the Shining Ones and our kindred elves is truly an intimate one.

If we were to view these Shining Ones from the perspective of the Angelic Hierarchy, they would be Thrones, Dominions, Virtues and so forth, for they deal with planets and regions of various dimensions that have ultimately sprung from their own being. That is to say have been a part of them at some point and have a natural affinity to them. Just as the cells that temporarily compose our bodies will one day/lifetime develop sentient awareness and be naturally inclined to assist us. Or perhaps obstruct us, depending on how we've treated them, so treat your body well.

The second group of Adepts work not as much with the direct development of *man* as with the Devas and the developing aspects and energies of the planet itself. In many ways their efforts are more long term, for the forces they deal with will sometimes evolve toward *human* consciousness but as yet are still allied closely to the mineral and animal kingdoms. They deal also with the elementals and other forces that function to support the efforts of the evolutionary progress of *humanity*. Again, if we can use the analogy of a film production, the difference is between the actors and what they do and the set designers, costume makers, composer and musicians etc. who support the production.

These adepts are more concerned with the awakening of the planetary centers and of the evolutionary progress of the planet itself, which has it own evolutionary destiny, than we elfin humanoid types who help populate it. These individuals work with occult forces, the subtle forces, and have less concern with charismatic powers that are so often needed for influencing humanoid elfin, as with the energies that move the planet and the beings on it as a whole. Thus, these individuals often tend to be introverted in nature, rather than extroverted as the teachers of *humanity* tend, and often need, to be. (For more on the evolution of crystals, gems and minerals on this planet we recommend *Healing Stoned* by Joel Glick and Julia Lorussa. A really great book.)

These adepts deal with the planet as a conscious being and help it come to a realization of its own nature and harmony within itself. This planet, like all of us on it, will in time die and be reborn as it pursues its own evolution. And remember that while most folks tend to think of the planet as merely a material sphere, it is an energetic being, with its own fate and destiny, as are we all.

The forces that these adepts wield are more in keeping with what is commonly considered magic by the mass of humanity, although they still wield them mostly on the unseen planes and not in the dramatic wand as lightening rod or ray-gun fashion of the movies.

Among these adepts you find those who continually chant, meditate and otherwise work for harmony in the world and they seek to unify the development of this planet, or whatever planet or plane they are upon, to the Cosmic order and often draw down forces from those great spheres in order to achieve this end.

It should also be obvious that the health of the planet is vital to those of us upon it while our own development can affect the progress of the psychic body of the planet, so there is an overlap, or a coordinated effort by the two sets of adept faerie folk to bring about this harmony. We depend upon each other, although clearly we depend on the planet much more than it needs us. However, understand that we are creating Elfin here. Manifesting Faerie. And when our work progresses the planet will radiate ever more brightly with elven magic and we will all benefit from the effects thereof.

We should note that the evolution of the planet has only incidentally to do with human evolution. The planet is vital to us, but again it has its own evolution and it will move on from us just as we will evolve from it. Still, the law of contact continues and once having been together there is an esoteric connection that will exist between us forever no matter how far we may wander from each other. And as much as we elves may love this planet, it is in our best interests and the best interests of the planet if we hasten our progress here and evolve to higher, or more subtle, dimensions as soon as we are able. This benefits us, and the planet, as well as all connected to it. Still though we are in many ways but temporary companions, it befits every elven adept to do their best in each and every situation and circumstances they may find thems'elves in. This is the eternal law of karma; we get what we put into things.

As part of this effort, these second type of adept elves frequently open thems'elves as channels for Universal energy so that the power and vibration of our galaxy will radiate through them. It is seldom that any one individual is powerful enough to have great effect in this regard, although that is possible, so most of these elves are very conscious of working en masse toward the goal. Thus you will often find them doing planetary mediations, or spells that are organized in which they merge their efforts with others of their persuasion, most of whom they've never meet but who, none-the-less, they know to be their cosmic and planetary colleagues.

It should be noted that those adepts who have evolved as spirits, but not as yet evolved soulfully, which is to say they seek their own selfish ends without regard to the needs of others or consideration for the harmony of the spheres, also draw down spirits from other regions to aid in their endeavors and it is this second group of adepts that generally must deal with these errant magics the soulfully un-evolved have called down, while the first group at times must deal directly with the dark sorcerers who summon them.

It is not wrong to seek one's own success, in fact that is only natural. It is the way we are designed. It is in our nature to do so. However, when we seek success ever at the expense of others and against the movement toward enlightened realization and upliftment, then we are acting contrary to the laws of the Universe and function as a sickness or a parasite within the planetary body. The goal is to cease being parasitic and to develop symbiotic relationships. In this way we achieve our own desire in harmony with the laws of the Universe and ultimate success becomes assured.

Such parasitic behavior is often tolerated for short periods; however, if the individual magician becomes a true danger to the whole he will eventually be eliminated from this sphere and reborn in the lower reaches of evolution where the dog-eat-dog instinct is a natural and accepted part of the evolutionary scheme. However, hope is continually held out that these spirits when faced with the reality of their actions and the karma that accrues therefrom will alter their direction, and get with the program, so to speak. To fail to do so is ultimately to wind up in an abyss with only one's own self as company.

Such major readjustments, however, tend to occur at periodic shifts of planetary and galactic reorientation when masses of spirits either rise to a new level or not. The Fall of Atlantis is an example of such a shift when one group rose and another fell. The End of the World predictions which tend to happen at least once a millennia, although thankfully inaccurate, the supposed Mayan Calendar predictions, all refer to just such a massive event even if the predictors are usually wrong. Although they may be accurate in a minor way since every lifetime has its own adjustments of karma and it is possible that those who predict the end of the world are in fact facing such a re-orientation in their coming life.

On the scale of an eon, we might call this graduation day. Some advance, some do not and must do the whole cycle over again, some are kicked out of school altogether that is to say demoted to a lower level of development. It is true that some spirits being strong, as they are, take advantage of this, even like it. They like being a big fish in a little pond, for their life experience does provide them with certain advantages; however, karmic limitations are also put upon them otherwise they would be stuck there nearly forever, or once again destroy their environment and sink to an even lower level of manifestation, which is not in their best interests nor anyone's else's.

From a materialistic point of view, you are what you appear to be. But from an elven point of view, a spiritual view, you are what you do. It is your magic, your action that really matters and shapes your future. Our current appearance, as well as our bodies, is a temporary manifestation of our spirit. Our spirit, however, while it does evolve will continually re-clothe, drawing new matter to itself. What is important is our energetic being that originates from our spirit and attracts to it energies that are attuned to such vibrations and thus manifest in the material world in keeping with that particular spirit under the limitations, or even you might say the authority, of our karma.

It is not wrong, as we have so indicated, to pursue one's own success, nor is one obligated to be utterly selfless and to serve without any personal reward. The goal is harmony of the small s'elf with the greater s'elf, the merging of the elf and Elfin, so that everyone is fulfilled perfectly. The problem with merely pursuing one's own happiness without concern for others is that it causes problems; it creates friction and disharmony, which obstructs the fulfillment of one's own goals. One winds up spending all one's time in conflict and one never really acquires the true peace and harmony one desires, nor the love, respect and admiration of others that most souls hunger to achieve.

Opting Out

Some folks, because of the difficulty of this world, and the stress of living in such primitive circumstances and amid such conniving spirits and egos struggling to succeed at everyone else's expense, contemplate, attempt or commit suicide. There is nothing karmically wrong with this; however, it is a useless effort. One merely starts again, faces the same trials and tribulations that drove one to suicide in the first place and eventually spirits come to realize this and that the way forward is much quicker than the way out. Why go through it two or three times if, with a bit of concerted effort and devotion, you really only have to endure it once? Using the analogy of college again, a particular life is like a required course necessary for one's graduation. Committing suicide is like dropping the course, which one can do, but it doesn't remove the obligation of completing the course to graduate. It just postpones the process.

So, too, there are those who come close to totally subjugating their ego, as they are so often told they must do by various religious doctrines and creeds, to devote thems'elves to service in the world. In a sense, this represents the suicide of their spirit. But like all suicides it is a temporary matter. It is quite possible that those who are attracted to this sort of egoless service were particularly selfish individuals in previous lifetimes and this is the only way to bring balance into their being by denouncing the ego personality, which is a function of their spirit, so their soul might be strengthened. However, for more advanced soulful spirits this abnegation of the spirit is neither necessary nor healthy. The Way is ever one of balance between the soulful and the spirited/spiritual, the many and the one merged, so the individual elf is indeed One with Everything, or really Everyone.

The Hierarchy of Evolutionary Elfhood

The following is a list of evolutionary stages that elves tend to go through after they have awakened. It is not at all necessary to progress through all these stages, which is to say one may in some cases skip stages, nor is it necessary to progress through all of them to the last stage. Our description of them is, shall we say, partial and theoretical and should not be taken as the whole or absolute truth. Each individual elf manifests in any particular stage in hir own fashion, but these are the general highlights.

1. The first stage is usually denoted by a sense of freedom from traditional societal boundaries and norms. The elf is aware that sHe belongs to a higher and more encompassing social system that is defined in many ways by hir own choices and beliefs. These elves, in a sense, make their own rules and as long as they don't violate the rules of the Universe and Karmic Laws of Inevitable Reaction this is not only fine but the way it is meant to be for they have a greater, more expansive, and freer understanding of life and its interconnections. This stage is usually celebratory and very s'elf indulgent and often denoted by the wise use of various drugs or intoxicants that are enlightening but non-addictive for the elf seeks by doing so to perpetuate hir connection to Faerie and the feeling of Elfin within her. It is also primarily a very sensual stage so usually a lot of fornication is associated with this stage. In fact, fornication in increasingly elegant and masterful ways can be seen in nearly every stage of elven development. However, being now free of the limitations of their upbringing the elf usually has no specific idea of where to proceed other than to enjoy life for all it's worth.

2. In the second stage of awakening the elf begins to make determined efforts to develop hirs'elf as a soul, spirit and particularly hir ability to interact with the material world. The mundane world is still very much in hir consciousness and sHe now seeks to Master it by mastering hir own body, mind and psyche. SHe may engage in various physical arts, such as karate, aikido, yoga, palates, as well as an increased awareness of diet, particularly proper nutrition. One tends at this point to consider vegetarianism, and if the elf doesn't choose

that at this point, sHe does tend to frequent health food stores, if sHe doesn't already and to eat organically. Also, elves very often meet each other or even find romance in health food stores. She may also develop interest in herbalism, acupuncture, and other forms of natural healing. SHe is very aware of s'elf actualization and pursues this course vigorously and sHe is increasingly aware of and attuned to the mind/body connection.

3. In the third stage of awakening the elfin spirit begins to seek and actively hang out with those on hir level or above. The third stage is an extension of the second stage in which second stage elves now exercise together, meditate together, and seek niches where their own kind frequent (including health food stores). Naturally, this is also the stage where elves tend to find mates, and often experiment with polyamorous relationships, and friends/elves with benefits and so forth. This stage, however, is still somewhat casual. There is often no specific commitment except for the commitment to help each other develop as elven spirits. There is something special about these elves and they feel this about thems'elves and their others. They are less inclined to hide from normal folk and more inclined to dance their elven dance for all to see. This does not mean they are unaware of the prejudices and biases that predominate in the world of the normals, but that they feel in control of their ability to reveal thems'elves or not as they choose in any particular circumstances for they also have developed an inner ability to recognize others of their kind almost instantaneously with whom they develop a subtle and almost unseen somatic language of touch. They may attempt to create an elven group or home but because of their basic independence, it is naturally going to be a very free

flowing environment where elves come and go and is most likely of a temporary and very bohemian nature.

4. The step from the third stage to fourth denotes a quantum leap in consciousness. The idea that the world is primarily a material event is replaced by the realization that the Universe is an energetic being and that this is not simply One world, one reality or one truth but that these are in many ways relativistic aspects of consciousness. One begins to perceive the reality of parallel worlds and dimensions and to understand that the way one experiences the world and how the world thus reacts to the individual depends greatly upon the way the individual chooses to experience the world. In this stage, this is a very mystic event. You find many channelers here, for one is in many ways overwhelmed by reality and sits back in awe of the possibilities that are so vast and profound that one is uncertain what to do with it all except watch the show and laugh. It is at this stage that one also often begins to see auras, stars floating or shooting past one through the walls of one's living room and other mystic phenomena. What can one say but, "Wow!" One begins to see, as well, that what makes us elven is not our genetic heritage but our spiritual heritage. We are not elves because of who are ancestors *were* but because of who we *are*.

5. The fourth stage yields, usually relatively quickly to the fifth stage, as the magic asserts itself. One begins to use one's choices to actively step from one parallel world to another realizing that all our decisions stem from world views and are therefore world experience choices and that while the parallel worlds are very similar, almost to the point of being nearly identical when they are very close to each other and overlap, that even the smallest choices can have long term consequences.

Understanding this, the elfin adept becomes ever more aware of hir actions and the effects of hir actions, and moves with caution through the world. This intense concentration and focus to each step will yield in time to elegant mastery of the Elven Way as one becomes increasingly aware of one's path, but for now such minute attention to small details is extremely important. Also, karma comes much more quickly at this stage and any deviation from the Way will find one nearly instantaneously warned, usually through what is often painful inconvenience, that one is in the process of "fucking up." However, as one progresses one learns the rules of this new and higher dimension of reality selection and such irritations caused by careless behavior are generally and easily avoided. At the same time, it is also full spend ahead. Realizing that one is creating one's own world, one's own eald, one's own region of Faerie and thus one's own reality, set the adept to doing just that and often at first at a feverish rate. Experience, however, tends to lead one to a more relaxed and casual, s'elf confident approach, as time and experience accumulates.

6. As always this new and higher understanding of reality is accompanied by an urge to unite with others of like heart, mind and vision. Alas, as one evolves beyond the mass of dominant humanity it becomes increasingly difficult to find others as evolved. Thus the elfin adept begins to look downward, seeking not only those who are on the same level of development but those who show the potential for increasing their intelligence and understanding to that higher level. The elf actively seeks to uplift hir others with an eye toward creating a community, commune, eald that is supportive of this reality and will stand as an independent force in the world. Thus one increasingly searches the ancient texts

for clues to magical realization, and also seeks to update these texts for their particular circumstances. One's magic becomes a way of life and one is a constant living vibration of attractive Fae energy. One is a beacon of Faerie and those seeking Faerie are naturally drawn to such a one. It is true that those who are not as yet so evolved will come and go from this advanced association but the adept understands this fact and does hir best to foster the elven nature of each individual as best sHe can for as long as the individual is around. In time, other adepts will appear who understand the Way and together they will create a ongoing eald that will eventually become a source/center of a whole new world.

7. Here another quantum leap occurs and the elf understands that sHe is at the forefront of an entire new species of being. Elves awakening within dormant human consciousness. At first one is overwhelmed by the realization that one is truly unique. This uniqueness naturally comes with increased magical powers and the elf is at first inclined to play around with this energy, seeking experience to see how it works and the extent of it. This is only natural and while in time the elf will become more cautious and less frivolous in using this energy, for learning purposes this light experimental approach is understandable. Once one gets used to one's new toy, one begins to understand that it is in fact a new tool and treats it with due respect, although that tends to come in the next stage. One, by this point, has bypassed all physical prejudices concerning elves as well as others. We no longer define ours'elves by pointed ears, style of clothes or race of origin; energetic spirit and conscious awareness alone define the elf. Nor do we pay much attention to the world's way of discrimination. It doesn't matter to us if a person is

Caucasian, Negroid, Oriental, from Europe, Africa, or the Far East, is Buddhist, Christian or Muslim or anything else. All that matters is: do they see what we see? And more importantly: do they wish to be our friends and cooperate toward mutual success and fulfillment? Living thus in a vaster world, naturally there are more opportunities for intimate interaction and the elf at this stage is inclined to indulge in those opportunities as much as possible.

8. While the elf releases the material distinctions that traditionally define what constitutes being an elf, sHe often feels a powerful contrast between hirs'elf and normal humanity, particularly those obstinate individuals who absolutely refuse to change or even consider facts, science, reason or logic as viable ways to examine ones'elf and understand the world. However, while the elf revels in hir "specialness" sHe in time comes to understand, in this 8th stage, that hir increasing power comes with responsibility for all those who come into hir purview, including those, perhaps ever particularly those, who are, by hir standards, evolutionarily challenged. These are the raw material from which sHe will create a new species and sHe begins increasingly to see individuals not for who they appear to be, but who they may become, that is the adept sees the potential, however meager, in each and every spirit. The adept elf also comes to understand, with increasing clarity, hir interconnection to the all of life and how we deeply affect our others by our actions. The adept thus begins to think on planetary, solar, and galactic scales of perception. The elf realizes as well that while hir body may fade that sHe is in reality an immortal spirit and this increased awareness and evolutionary development tends to extend hir life and to act to make hir age less quickly.

9. In the ninth stage one increasingly takes one's place among the Shining Ones. Some might view this like monks in a religious order, and it has that quality, but within this there is an intimacy, an erotic, ecstatic hum of relationship that makes this interaction orgasmic. At this stage, the adept elf passes from the material world altogether and increasing takes one's place in Faerie, touching this world only from afar via their enchantments and other magic. The adept elf, this Shining One, creates hir own realm of Faerie and unfolds hir Vision in the world, which is primarily composed of the cells, atoms, and other substances that once composed hir various bodies (and in a sense still do) through the lifetimes. Only now hir body is of cosmic dimension. The Dance of Life goes ever on and the sensuous interplay of the Adepts creates magic that unfolds eternally. You are bound to encounter some young elf who claims, in an desperate hunger for s'elf importance and recognition, that sHe has already achieved this stage of development, and certainly sHe has done so, imaginally if in no other fashion, and are thus destined to do so more fully as hir lives develops. The Shining Ones, ever eager to empower the potential of all elves, will certainly note this ambition and send these elves the trails and quests needed to help them achieve this goal.

10. How can we describe this being? This radiant, charismatic elfin spirit who lights up every dimension sHe crosses. SHe is healing, sHe is eternally youthful, and compared to us SHe is a God. SHe no longer consumes. SHe is s'elf nourished and s'elf sustaining. SHe gives forth energy but never needs to take it from others because SHe is always hirs'elf spreading outward and contracting again unto hirs'elf. SHe is the Magic playing. Creating the Worlds, Dimensions and

Universes. SHe is One with Faerie. Playfully Eternal. Joyous forever. And will only pass from this world when SHe becomes bored, which SHe almost never does, and submerges hirs'elf into it again, like a child asking its parent to read that bedtime story one more time. SHe knows that it is not the goal but the journey that is the true destination and SHe journeys forever. If you encounter such a One it will be in terms of a blessing in your life, a bit of relief, a comic accident of good luck. You will be amazed; and if wise, you will be thankful.

11. This being is totally dedicated to hir creation. Parallel worlds and dimensions issue from hir consciousness and sHe exists as the magic within the worlds we know. SHe at this point is still linked to us, in a sense, although sHe is far beyond us and functions on time scales that would seem nearly infinite to us. SHe is One with Faerie and has such powerful control over hirs'elf, which is to say is so profoundly evolved that hir every thought comes to, what to us would seem to be, instantaneous realization. At the same time, what we consider thought, is a very slow and complex process compared to hir thought, which is direct, creatively imaginative, vision oriented and is a direct expression of hir being. We live in hir Universe. We are part of hir body. We follow in hir footsteps and one day shall be as sHe while sHe moves on to even greater realization.

12. Here these great beings gather and merge to create vaster worlds than any could create alone. Note that the worlds they create are often composed of the atoms of their previous bodies, as mentioned, and the others of their kind with which they are now linked were often friends, lovers, companions, parents, children and others karmically connected to them in the past. These

links of association are never undone and even if one parted on poor terms in the past that doesn't sever the connection. The hope always is that through evolution the individuals involved will have progressed and matured enough to make a greater success of relationships they so pitifully trashed in past lives. We cannot say exactly what these individuals do together, for it is a creative process and surprising things often manifest therefrom; but we know that it is amazing beyond our limited imaginations.

13. Beyond that we cannot, at this point at least, really know. The individuals who attain this 13th stage function in a world that is at or beyond the speed of light and thus utterly inaccessible to us. We can only fantasize what it might be like and approximate from the seeds, which are our own s'elves, that will eventually reach these great heights of being. We expect that the cycle of evolution goes ever on and that in coming this far one is ever closer to the Source that is the Magic from which all potential realizes its'elf.

> *"WE ARE ALL RETURNING TO ELFIN FROM DIFFERENT DIRECTIONS AND THE PATH THAT IS RIGHT FOR YOU MAY BE THE WRONG WAY FOR ANOTHER."*
> —*THE SILVER ELVES*

The Elven Way

The many realms of Faerie
Weave together well
Seamlessly united
By a loving spell
Of beauty most creative
Of friendship ever true
Of fairness done to every one
Where each receives his due
The elves in trees that sparkle
The faeries gliding by
The pixies with their many games
The nymphs with longing sighs
The Shining Ones most regal
Pass by on their parade
And even when they're lost from sight
The memory does not fade
For once one's touched by Elfin
Or been to where they dwell
The slightest hint
Or passing scent
Will make one's heart to swell

CHAPTER 8:
HARMONIC ATTUNEMENT

We are the magical channels for those ideas, ideals and individuals whose example in various forms inspires us. We mix and merge these energies and make them our own by developing our own style, just as a painter might copy a Master to learn from hir work but will only master painting when sHe develops and perfects hir own style. There are, for example, those who can copy a Master perfectly (such as art forgers), but that doesn't make them masters. Unique style is essential to mastery. It is not merely a matter of the perfection of technique but of contributing something truly creative to the world. Thus in following the Way of the elfin magician adepts who have gone before us we must ever take the vibrational magic we have received and make it our own. In that way only do we truly contribute to the magic of the world. And this is ever what Faerie encourages and requires of us.

However, to receive these vibrations from Faerie we must become ever more attuned to it while not losing, in fact strengthening, our own vibrational energy. In a certain sense it is impossible to not put ours'elves into our magic; but there are times, particularly in the early stages, when we are trying so hard to receive the energy correctly that we lose connection with ours'elves and the vibration we emit is not entirely on key, so to speak. Thus we strive to do two essential things at the same time, that is receive the pure vibration of Faerie and at the same time allow it to play through our instrument, our being, as we increasingly learn to attune that instrument. What is our instrument? It is our mind, body, feelings, soul and spirit. These are the instruments of our being; the instruments of our magic.

They are the true wands, chalices, blades, and pentacles of our magical art.

Means of Attuning

The means of attuning ours'elves is multifold. Being near or in contact and association with those elves who are further along on the path than we is always helpful, for not only do we learn from their vibrations and example but they serve to inspire us to continue on the path.

We may also strive with others on our same level, but being at the same stage of development this can entail greater struggle; however, we do tend to buoy each other and what challenges we face are balanced by the joy of mutual learning and association. We also can, and most elves do, have mystical connection to the Harmony of Faerie and the vibration of at least one Shining One. But any way we chose, or a combination thereof, the merging of these ways being optimal, we still have the obligation of developing our own s'elves, our own minds, bodies, spirits, souls and feelings or emotional psychological maturity. It is just that in good company this is made easier, and alone it often tends to be more difficult, but the process is essentially the same.

This development of the s'elf includes the clearing of karmic debts and the accumulation of possible magic that rebounds to one's benefit. Most of all it involves the transformation of our habits of thought, feeling, response, reaction, will and behavior. One cannot pursue the Elven Way without in time becoming both thoroughly transformed while becoming at the same time closer and closer to one's true and natural s'elf: innocent without being naïve, childlike without being foolish, joyous without dissipation, and dedicated without turning pompous and arrogant. Magic is not always an easy art until we take it and make it easy.

The Elven Way

Just as a tone sounded will vibrate the related strings on a piano, harp or other string instrument, so do the Magic of Faerie and the Shining Ones and their vibration pluck a cord within our elven being. The more attuned we become, that is the more in tune with our own natures and with greater Nature, the more easily this happens and the more likely that those great beings with whom we are destined to associate will be able to channel power through us. We are not blind channels in this, however, but conscious colleagues who take this raw power that we are given and use it creativity to fulfill the vision as we see and experience it. Still, one must be truly ready for this influx of power for this magical energy will test the clarity of our being and the strength of our psychic and etheric body. Those who are not ready for such powerful energy become ill or go a little crazy for a while but in most cases this is but a minor problem, merely a way of making the individual strive a bit harder to clear hir karma and develop hir vehicles.

As the adept elf develops, hir ability to channel these energies, to refocus them according to need and circumstance, grows ever greater. We may think of this like a government grant of funds to use for the creative arts. The artist gets the grant but it is up to the artist to create according to hir own vision. And, of course, in most cases the more developed the artist becomes, the more likely sHe is to receive a grant, but family association is almost always a factor both on Earth and among the Stars. It is not just about what you know and your ability to use that knowledge, but also who you know. Of course, every true artist will go on creating whether they receive a grant or not, but the grant does provide one with the time and the tools to do something truly amazing, although one is also generally instilled with a sense of responsibility to produce something truly great. But then what artist doesn't strive to produce greatness in every work they create?

All of us, whether elves or not, whether pursuing the Elven Way, the Christian faith, or some other way, or no path at all, are still bombarded by influences from the planetary and cosmic forces, as well as the pressures of the world that are the subsequent manifestation of those forces. But by pursuing the Elven Way, one is directly invoking and evoking these forces in an amplified fashion and the pressure subsequently builds. Only those who have worked upon their s'elves and who continue to do so are prepared for this tremendous influx of energy.

The forms and techniques of this channeling vary. Some, like Buddhist monks, meditate and channel the energy into the world in that way. Christian monks pray. Both chant (the source of the word enchantment) in resonant tones, sending forth a vibration through sound, thought, feeling and intention into the world. Magicians summon spirits and set them forth to fulfill their will. Sorcerers use subliminal suggestion to affect the behavior of others. And there are other ways as well, esoteric ways, such as speaking to individuals' subconscious through the light in their eyes. We elves use all these techniques and more. However, all of them, and we know we have said this previously but it is vitally important, all of them depend upon the development and maturity of the individual elf. Working on ours'elves, developing ours'elves, our abilities and our powers, is key to everything.

While on the lower levels of initiation, that is the first two levels of initiation, the training is essentially the same, so much so that one can even, and by the nature of things many do, begin one's training under the auspices of the Unseelie or even the Demonic, or vice versa. Those who ultimately chose the path of dominance and subjugation have also often begun their training among the forces of enlightenment and illumination. As one proceeds to the third initiation and beyond, one must make a clear choice (or relatively clear choice) between the two basic uses of one's powers. Also, as one proceeds, this similarity of training gives way increasingly to specialization. Like a scholar gaining higher and higher degrees tends to choose a particular branch of hir field to specialize within, so too do adepts tend to choose a particular aspect of evolutionary development to actualize. However, also like scholars, which

The Elven Way

we truly are, only of an occult and esoteric variety, that doesn't mean we discontinue our education concerning the more general aspects of our field of study or cease studying other branches of knowledge.

However, specialization is necessary for the most part if one is to accomplish something worthwhile. One must become intimate with one's field, so to speak; and it is a tendency of our own natures to individuate, to increasingly define ours'elves and our spirits. Also, the Universe and Faerie are so vast that while one may become One with Faerie, to create anything one must still reach down into the mundane, stirring the energies in particular areas and by various means.

The first and foremost of these choices is again between those who choose to work with evolving humanity and from these will come its teachers, and are thus those who awaken the spirit in elves and in others. The other choice is to follow the path of those who work with planetary forces overall, becoming those elves, who are in essence as we've explained, imaginally often pictured as flower faeries, working with the elementals, the flora, fauna, minerals and other elements of planetary and eventually Solar initiation and beyond.

Also, while some deal with the evolution of the planet, or the various souls and spirits associated with it at this point, there are those who have a connection to inter-stellar groups who are being prepared to participate in cosmic life and their true contribution, after long lives of training, will only come far, far in the future. Understand that the evolution on this planet is not occurring in isolation; we are connected to an evolving galaxy and cosmic system and there are forces at play that affect our own evolution with these greater connections in mind. Many of those individuals who are destined to function in these greater realms probably seem to ordinary humanity as extremely shy, or introverted, maybe even a bit crazy, as they seem to have almost no interest in what is going on in the mundane world around them. Many of those who are labeled autistic fall into this category.

Those individuals who tend toward dealing with solar and stellar forces are generally of another type. They tend to care less about the material concerns that intrigue most folks and instead are fascinated by the movement of energy over vast arenas. Often you will find these adepts developing their abilities in high-energy business or government circles. These spirits are often action oriented and love functioning in high stress situations.

Plus there are those soulful spirits who have migrated here, for particular lessons, from other stellar systems, and these often appear unique, or peculiar to much of humanity. There are, for instance, sea people from distance galaxies who have an incredible affinity for the ocean and who always seem to just naturally float whenever they are in the water. There are also sea sprites and mer-folk, mermaids and lads, who in this dimension must live on land and develop various aspects of their spirit by doing so. Again, these folks tend to have a never-ending longing for the sea or water. Inland, you may find them forever hanging around rivers, lakes and swimming pools.

Understand that everything material is energy. $E=MC^2$. There is consequently also a lot of *free* energy available; what one might call wasted energy, and the adept elf is able to amass this energy and redirect it toward the magical purposes sHe envisions. Thus elves, for the most part, do not waste much energy. We as adepts become ever more efficient in our actions and our movements.

We should remind you that when we speak of soulful spirits, we are not merely anthropomorphizing. We don't imagine that every spirit is humanoid. Rather, we are animists. All of life, all matter, which is to say all energy, is alive, that is has a form of awareness, and has spirit and consciousness in its particular form. The trees are spirits, the rocks are spirits, the wind is a spirit and all else is as well. So it is important to realize that there are developing tree adepts, Tolkien's Ents are an allusion to this fact, developing rock spirits, and so forth. So, too, the Shining Ones do not necessarily have human bodies, although they are of such a high level of magical ability that they could if they so desired. They are, rather, shape-shifters, or energy shifters and can formulate their energy into any form or vehicle that they find convenient for their purposes at a particular time. Mostly however, we might think of them, and this with practical reasons, as beings of light, for that is what they truly are.

Those who train on a planetary level often specialize in developing powers with a particular elemental. There are those who work with water, those who train with fire, air or earth elementals. In a sense, you might say that the elemental is their body, at least temporarily, and they are the consciousness of that body. However, it should be noted that even in the human body, while the brain dominates, the stomach also has a sort of mind, and the rest of the body does as well. This is due to the fact that the whole of the being, every atom is in the process of evolutionary development and will in time become consciously aware as an independent spirit.

Water is an especially powerful elemental on this planet and those who work with it also tend to develop energies having to do with the feelings and psychic perceptions. This is heightened by the fact that so much of the human body is composed of water, although while this tends to indicate that these adepts are involved primarily with human feelings and psychic perception, it would be a mistake to limit our understanding simply to human interaction.

Fire is another primary elemental and from its interaction with water comes air. The Fire adepts are energizing while the Water adepts can be very soothing, although they can also be tumultuous if they so choose although that usually involves influence from the fire, air or earth elementals.

Air adepts have great power in the intellectual realm and can be quite inspiring due to this. Air and fire together, that is in a certain sense to say oxygen, awaken the spirit. Those who work with Earth often begin their adept-ship by studying as sculptors, learning to shape physical manifestation. From these ideas one can extrapolate for even greater understanding. The Fire adepts, for instance, are closely allied with solar light and thus develop a profound influence throughout the solar system and eventually move on to the galactic sphere.

Other elves deal with devas, who are to our minds advanced faeries; or deal directly and intimately with the Shining Ones, who most folks would conceive of as angelic beings. Some work with the demonic folks. That is to say they keep these anti-evolutionary forces in line and limit their effect. Naturally, they work very hard to help counteract the destructive tendencies that Man has developed since he parted from his Pagan roots and pre-pagan, pre-religious shamanic magical practices, and abandoned his active cooperation with the devas and with Nature. This tendency to believe Mankind rules Nature and can do anything he desires without consequence is an effect of listening to demonic forces who take active glee in man's destructive tendencies that will ultimately enslave him to them.

Fortunately for mankind, many of the occult centers have been sealed off while he develops his scientific and rational mind. It may thus seem to him that there is no such thing as magic, which for much of humanity is currently true. This, however, is a temporary situation to help keep man from destroying himself, which he would likely do if he had access to these esoteric powers. For elves, this closing of the occult centers has made things a bit more difficult, but for us it is like weightlifting, we are building up our magical muscles in this era when the occult energies are more sparse and limited. When the shift comes into the sixth sub-race, this barrier will pass and we will once again have full access to the energy of the planet and the solar and inter-stellar realms.

Others study to take their place among the Lords of Karma,

who balance all things in time. These limitations of karma, however, are not really punishments, as many presume, but the necessary consequence of our own behavior in this and previous lifetimes. The Lords of Karma are merely acting on our own behalf to enforce those limitations that we have, in effect, set upon ours'elves according to the behavior, direction, and magic we have chosen to pursue, although it should be noted that in the lower levels, before initiation, this choice is often an unconscious one.

One need not concern ones'elf overly with what specialized path one will pursue. The fact is if we follow our natural instincts we will find the right way, becoming ever more our own true s'elves. This is not the military. We are not assigned willy-nilly here or there without any consideration for our own talents or desires, although it is true that sometimes we are faced with challenges meant to deepen and expand our understanding, lest we unknowingly limit ours'elves without thorough understanding. We are elves and our kindred, our family, who are the Shining Ones, wish the best for us and always act with that in mind. You may think of the Shining Ones as very intelligent, enlightened and good parents ever seeking to do what is best for their children, although they tend to think of thems'elves as elder brothers and sisters.

Some elven adepts work particularly with their chosen ethnic group and try to bring understanding there. Others work with the evolution of humanity as a planetary people and attempt to influence all groups toward planetary consciousness. Others still serve as a connection between these two groups, working with a particular ethnic group, or a couple of related ethnicities, while promoting higher elven planetary consciousness. This is in part why elves in a particular culture often still hold a powerful feeling of, and love for, the culture they've been raised within even though they see and function beyond it. This is as it is meant to be. What is important, however, is that we do all we can to soothe the conflicts that are so often enculturated in individuals of one group against other groups.

We elves are bridge builders, seeking to bring understanding between estranged peoples. Elven adepts are aware that we are all genetically related, not only to other humans but all other creatures on this planet.

Group Participation

If you get involved in a group that tells you to forgo your ego and surrender to what the leader, guru, god, in other words what they tell you to do, you have probably fallen in with the wrong crowd. This is not to say you can't learn from these. For as we've mentioned, on the lower levels of initiation the training is essentially the same, but in the long run as an elf you have to realize that to truly evolve you also have to take responsibility for your own magic, and if you follow others it is important that you do so because you see and embrace the wisdom and illumination of their vision, not because you've been harassed and coerced into doing so.

Free departure is important as well. Do they try to make you feel like you will fail or be cursed if you leave the group? Free choice is always an essential aspect of the Elven Way, and the sincere are always welcome among us; and those who intuitively are drawn to another way are farewell-ed with blessings and our abiding love, as well as an invitation to return. You are always welcome home.

Lest we despair, it should be noted that mankind's alienation from Nature is an expected event that is in keeping with the development of his intellectual capacity, which is temporarily separated from his soulful feeling aspect for a (relatively) short time. This is an accepted period in fifth root race evolution and as the sixth sub-race of the fifth root race, which is the precursor to the sixth root race, begins to function in the Aquarian Age, which is to say more and more Fae folk awaken, the merging of the mental and feeling aspects in the form of intuitional and psychic development will ameliorate this

The Elven Way

alienation of Man and Nature. Naturally, we elves, being of a higher initiation for the most part, and having in many cases been through this whole process on another stellar system, do not have to go through this again (except in the form of recapitulation prior to our first Saturn Return) and are often appalled to see men callously cut down trees, and pollute the air and sea, but we realize as well that this is in part why we are here so we may help transform this situation and inspire normal folk toward more enlightened understanding, and therefore behavior, in the world. Thus when elves depart from us it is not only with an understanding that they are, hopefully, pursuing the intuitive path of their spirit, but also that they may very well need to leave for awhile to learn certain lessons and we will quite likely see them again farther down the road.

It is true that most of us at this point simply seem to be trying to figure out what we are going to have for supper. But this confusion and uncertainty concerning mundane affairs is often found among those whose vision is ever toward the future and seek in all we do, as much as possible, to use our magic to create a better world. And, it needs to be said, even those who are simply involved in day-to-day life are also in training, their future specialization revealed by their current tendencies, interests and behaviors. In other words, in the long run we are all on the path of evolution; we can't help being who we are, and inevitably in time become who we are truly meant to be. Meant to be by whom? Why our own true s'elves, ever becoming.

> "THE ELVES ARE OF THE OPINION THAT THE SUN GETS UP FAR TOO EARLY IN THE MORNING. WE'D NEVER TELL HIM THAT, BUT WE DO TRY TO SET A BETTER EXAMPLE."
> —ELVEN WORDS TO LIVE BY

As we attune to Faerie bright
We become that Elven light
That burns on through the darkest night
Guiding kindred home
In the forest deep we glow
Shedding light that all souls know
Comes from seeds that magics sow
Spread by elf and gnome
In every fairy tale its shed
And to the world it is thus wed
This is the truth that's ever said
In esoteric tome
No matter if you wander far
Or you forget you have a star
Or covered yet by karma's tar
Or deep in ocean foam
We soon will get you back with us
Clean you up and make a fuss
Even listen to you cuss
And every hair will comb
For you're ours that's always clear
Whether distant or quite near
You need not have a bit of fear
Beneath the sheltered dome
Of our enchanted OM.

CHAPTER 9:
THE MAGIC OF THE SHINING ONES

*A*s the awakened elf takes on greater initiation and begins to function creatively in cooperation with the Shining Ones and with Faerie itself, which is to say the Source, the great Magic, hir magical growth is quickened by the increased power and the intensity of the forces that sHe now uses for hir magical creations. Naturally, this causes a rapidity of evolutionary development that will not be found in your average normal person who most often not only doesn't embrace change, as the adept elf does, but actively avoids it, in fact, is in many ways terrified by its possibilities. This acceptance of new energies and possibilities by the elf, tends to arouse here-to-fore un-accessed parts of hir being, awakening latent talents, powers and abilities. Remember most humans only use a small portion of their brain capacity, and this increase in energetic connection tends to illuminate greater portions of our brains. In time, this development will prove evolutionarily significant.

There are a number of effects of this evolutionary initiatory development for the adept elf, the first of which is that since the elf's powers are being heightened, the elf thus has more power to do good, as well as being faced with greater temptation, which is to say opportunity, to misuse this power. This is where the development of magical maturity becomes so very important. The elf comes to understand that magic is the use of will power to create effects in the world, but also that initiation requires the development of magical and enlightened intent. It is not enough to be able to create change according to one's will, one needs to create the type of change that will rebound positively for hir and all others and bring hir ever closer to Faerie by increasing hir awareness of and actualization of hir own true s'elf.

Another effect, and this is an effect of growing maturity, is that the elf has a maximized increase in experience compared to most folks. That is to say that the elf experiences in a few years what others often take a lifetime to experience. This is in part why we so often are called old souls, and in fact, this is in part a result of having been through much of this in previous incarnations and are often recapitulating those lifetimes in this one, thus moving through such experiences much more quickly than a normal person tends to do.

But also this is an effect of our increased vibrational rate in addition to our greater understanding of life and the occult, magical and mystical aspects of life. We process experiences more quickly and have less of a tendency to cling to things we have endured. We are more flexible, adaptable and less resistant to change. We are less likely to struggle with change and more likely to try to shape it to our intent. We always take with us what is valuable for us from our experience, but we are ever moving onward. Also, due to the increased vibrational frequency, we attract those who bring us even more experiences, greater knowledge and understanding. In part, this is a consequence of having cleared much of our karma and having set our course in such a way as to minimalize accumulating more negative karma, and when we do happen to do so, that is take a wrong karmic turn, we deal with it quickly, making adjustments and reparations as soon as we are able.

Here also comes, with increasing clarity, the realization that our personal Destiny and the Destiny of all beings on our particular planetary system are in most cases intimately entwined. The threads of fate, karma and destiny hold us together lifetime after lifetime. And it is at this point that the adept elf begins to realize that the development of her power and abilities, the increasing power of her true s'elf, is not only in her own best interest, but in keeping with the true interest of everyone else as well. Thus it is also at this time that the elf plunges hirs'elf near totally into development of hir personal powers. SHe hungers to be greater, to have power in the world, and as long as sHe holds steadfast to hir intent, hir vision and the Elven Way, this is a natural and favorable advance in hir progress. This after all is the test. It is not just about increasing one's magical and other powers in a world that is, shall we say, magically challenged at this time, but being able as spirits to hold to the greater vision and not fall for the illusion, the maya, that is the world as it appears to be, and therefore become entangled in the endless fulfillment of desires without any understanding of the true goal that we seek to actualize. One must be aware not only of this lifetime, but the progress of what is called liåle in Arvyndase, or samsara in Buddhist philosophy, that is the progress of our soulful spirit through the lifetimes.

This is also where meditation is often helpful in developing the inner calm that promotes this increased evolutionary activity. Naturally, when the elf first awakens sHe pursues hir quest with an impassioned fervor wanting to make as much progress as rapidly as possible, and in many cases to make up for what one often feels to be lost time, as well as put as much distance between ones'elf and normal humanity as possible. However, such impassioned early beginnings often give way to the abandonment of the quest and disillusionment with the limitations of one's progress and those that endure on the path do so because they develop a serenity of feeling that aids them to persevere without becoming frustrated with slow progress.

One comes in time to see that this is a long, long quest that we have been upon for lifetimes and will be for lifetimes yet to come and really, seen in that light, there is no great hurry or urgency if one does one's best in each and every moment. In many ways, this is about giving up our expectations and replacing them with a steady determination on the path and illuminating them with the understanding that one is in this for the long haul. This is not a fad having to do with this particular incarnation; it is the ongoing quest to fulfill our destiny as soulful spirits through Eternity.

Some of us, upon first awakening and being granted a vision of Faerie and the future, take a vow to follow the Elven Way till all our kindred are awakened and we manifest Elfin upon the Earth, in Space and among the Stars. This is a voluntarily oath. Such a vow is always taken at the elf's own initiation and request. However, while many mean it at the time they create and take this oath, few keep to this vow. And that is all right. They are simply not ready to devote thems'elves fully to the path of initiation, and we understand that. There is no penalty to abandoning this quest, save the natural penalty of straying from the path and thus missing the opportunities for development and the connection to Faerie it offers. In many ways, and for many folks, it is like leaving a lover only to realize later in life what a foolish act abandoning them proved to be.

So, too, many come to understand that in abandoning the Elven Way they discarded something precious, a jewel beyond price, although it can always be found again. We are ever awaiting our kindred and welcome them with our whole hearts when they return. But for those who hold such vows sacred and keep to them despite all temptation, frustration and moments of wavering, the rewards are many and the magic accumulates and manifests in ways that astound the normal folk, who think us especially lucky and blessed, which we are.

This determination of one's path upon the Way is accompanied by the maturity of the soulful elfin spirit. This is to say one gradually, and usually through persistent effort, overcomes one's tendency to become easily angered, frustrated, disillusioned, deceived by empty and meaningless enthusiasm, or whatever one's personal weaknesses may be. Over time we cease to be reactionary beings, that is merely pawns to the actions of others, and become beings of action. Our actions are natural, springing from the well of our inner being, but seldom dependent upon the actions of others. If someone should insult us or offend us, we don't necessarily respond immediately with insult in turn, nor do we necessarily turn away from them. Our actions are ever in keeping with our Vision and designed to respond to others in such a way as to achieve the higher goals toward which we aspire. Of course, we elves are not perfect beings, but beings who are perfecting ours'elves and if, at times, we fail to live up to our higher standards, this simply makes us resolve ours'elves to do better the next time.

We are in a state of constant training and like most students, we still have a lot to learn. This training is mostly s'elf inspired, a constant vigil over our own inner s'elves, our minds, our emotions, our behaviors and so on. It is mostly about developing our s'elves and maturing as soulful spirits, as personalities, however, as we point out, it also bears the incipient magical paths that we ultimately follow, of healing, channeling, world building, or energy working in various modes and techniques.

Like all advanced students, our education is mainly s'elf initiated. We pursue the path because we desire to improve ours'elves, but the Shining Ones, who are always on the outlook for talented individuals to assist them, in addition to empowering all spirits as best they may, ever seek to aid us in this effort. To do this they send us dreams, visions, and various magical experiences, often appearing in the form of synchronicities to guide us. One thing leads to another and when one advances upon the path one finds this increasingly true, with few gaps and less waiting between experiences that those on lower levels of initiation often encounter as they rush eagerly forward, often before they are truly ready for the next step in their education causing delays that they find so frustrating. This is the school of life and while it may have recess, and have summer vacations; it is an education that never ends.

Levels of Initiations

The Initiations are linked to the chakras and to the seven rays of manifestation and by examining the influences of these aspects one can come to understand the process of our development.

1. The First Initiation is at its root connected to the urge to survive that is linked with the first chakra. For the elf, this means not only developing financial independence in the world, but first and foremost, developing a sense of the independence, a sense of s'elf worth, and the right to think for ones'elf, to choose one's own direction. Thus in time this initiation also leads to the growth of leadership abilities. By that we do not necessarily mean authority, which is to say power over others, but becoming an example, an exemplar, that inspires others to pursue their own elven path. The first initiation gives one a basic grip on making a living in the world, of supporting ones'elf; however, it should be noted that for some advanced adepts, the Shining Ones temporarily take care of this aspect by sending others to provide the support the elf needs to fulfill hir particular mission.

2. The Second Initiation is in its lowest level about making contact and connection with others. It demands the most basic ability to cooperate with others and fulfills the need that nearly all individuals experience to interact with other beings. It develops into the power to draw others toward one. Thus it involves the development of attraction, particularly but not exclusively erotic attraction for it also involves the energy by which one requires and attains friends, allies and companions on

the Way. After the elf awakens, discovers hir true nature and confirms hir right to pursue hir own direction in life, sHe almost immediately hungers to share this with others like hir and therefore actively seeks hir kindred. This second initiation establishes hir power to succeed in that quest. In its higher aspects this power develops into compassion and true and unattached love, which is to say love without expectation.

3. The Third Initiation involves an expansion of power. It also involves the acquisition of knowledge. The elf believes in hir path and pursues it with hir kindred, now sHe desires and begins to demand to get at least basic recognition from others on other spiritual paths. To do this, however, sHe finds sHe has to acquire the knowledge to explain the path in a way that these others will comprehend, as well as, explain it to other elves who are also seeking. What is the Elven Way? How is it distinguished from various religions, and how does one follow, or pursue, this path? Thus the elven adept becomes increasingly able to answer these questions, establish hir own eald in the world, and create a secure place for the kindred to live and gather? To do this sHe often delves deeply into the magical, religious, mystical, spiritual, occult, and esoteric traditions from cultures all over the world, eclectically adapting everything of value to hir own needs and transforming all into hir elven understanding.

4. The Fourth Initiation follows the work of the third initiation of synthesizing all one encounters into an understanding of the world and of Faerie. This fourth initiation is harmonizing in nature. It understands that all differences are differences of appearance and essential for the value of aesthetics and that beneath all

things the Universe is One. The elf sees the Universe and the world as a full palette of colors with each culture and every dimension contributing to the infinite possibility of the beauty of creation. The impulse of this fourth level is both one of blending and creativity, and it is here that the elven adept firmly begins to express hir own unique contribution to elven philosophy, lore and, in time, history.

5. The Fifth Initiation introduces the elven adept to the more subtle dimensions of the Shining Ones and the elf begins to truly specialize, that is plunge in depth into the aspects and powers that sHe has, heretofore, been exploring. SHe finds that all the skills and talents sHe has been developing heretofore merge into a unique talent, or really style, that is her very own. SHe takes hir place among the planetary builders and maintainers, or among the great teachers, scientists or inventors of humanity, and begins to affect the consciousness of the human race as a whole. SHe becomes a shaper of worlds.

6. The Sixth Initiation finds the elven adept harmonizing hir creation with other creations. Hir eald takes its place, shall we say in an intimate and loving fashion, among the other realms of Faerie. At this point the elf is beyond what we normally think of as human, and functions in dimensions that are in many ways only tenuously connected to the mundane plane. However, these adepts are connected and oversee the development of the Sixth Root Race, which is an elven race more on the lines of the nearly immortal elves that Tolkien envisioned. They also oversee the sixth-sub race of the fifth root race, the precursor to the sixth root race (and in fact every sixth sub-race), which is just now beginning to manifest on the earth bringing Elven

light and magic into the world.

7. With the Seventh Initiation one truly enters the realm of the Shining Ones, those angelic elven beings of light who are pure sentient energy. These individuals oversee the future of evolution but in such a distant time and fashion that they are beyond our understanding without extending our minds intuitively beyond the limitations of the mundane world entirely. They might be conceived of as pure light, pure love, and pure being. They are unique stars in the starry universe. They oversee the evolution of the seventh root race, those being who will gradually become beings of light, and therefore also oversee the development of the seventh sub-race of every previous root race, which are the precursors for the seventh root race.

Realms of Magic Initiation

Understand that you are ever and always an independent agent of the Divine Elven Magic, and that while one may have achieved a certain level of initiation it doesn't mean that one is finished developing on the levels previous to it. We are continually advancing on every level we have achieved; for initiation is just that, a beginning, an introduction to a realm of power and development that we are then free to explore and expand upon. Initiation provides an entryway, a key to a new level of power, but it is up to the individual adept to make the most of the opportunities that one encounters on this new and higher region. Naturally, one must become increasingly stable as an individual to handle the intense amount of power that one begins to handle. This is especially true concerning one's inner s'elf, which is to say one's emotional and psychological being, that in coordination with the imaginal aspects of the mind, the determination of the will, and the vision guided intent, accumulates and expresses (magically) enormous occult power.

Naturally, this evokes one's soul for it is via the soul that one connects to all that is around one, and in this way is able to accumulate and store the free energy, or magic, that exists in the world and in Nature. Without this soulful connection this accumulation of energy is both limited and stilted and requires in many ways almost as much energy to accumulate it, as one is able to glean from the environment.

However, besides these occult energies, the adept most often has to deal with the world as it is, both because of hir particular karma as an individual and also because sHe is descending into the world in order to uplift others, in the same way that a doctor, say, may go into the slums to help treat the poor and diseased. Many elves, particularly those who are recently awakened, simply want to escape from the world, and that is understandable and it is their right to do so if that is their choice. They may need to escape for a while. We don't judge. But for some the work is here, the quest is here, and here, too, is the great adventure.

Naturally, on all levels of initiation the adept strives, indirectly really, to develop wisdom in dealing with these increased powers and abilities. We say indirectly because a direct attempt at the acquisition of wisdom is seldom effective and often results in the individual deceiving hir own s'elf, as well as sometimes attempting to deceive others, about how wise sHe is. Instead, the adept focuses on hir vision and the guiding principles of the Way and allows wisdom to overtake hir in its own time.

There is also the continual development of discrimination. We don't, of course, mean prejudice, but we do mean that the adept carefully considers how sHe will invest hir energy, financial to magical, and whom sHe will empower and invest in. Naturally, we are courteous to all who come to us, and every individual who crosses our path looking for upliftment gets a blessing. But most of all, as the adept elven progress, we invest most of our time and energy into those advanced beings through whom we will touch many other lives. We don't spend a lot of time or energy on those who are not yet ready to receive and use the magic we have to offer. Such would be a waste of their time as well as our own. Thus we are ever on the look out for advancing elven adepts, on whatever level, and do all we can to aid them.

Compassion does not demand we throw away our time or energy endeavoring to help those who don't really wish our assistance, or who will only dissipate what we give them without any effort to improve themselves and their lot. At the same time, there are times when we are moved to help someone, to give money to a homeless person or a beggar, for instance, knowing that they will probably waste what we give them on drugs or alcohol, but we don't concern ours'elves with that. We don't judge them, nor try to figure out whether they will use the money well or not. In those moments, when we are drawn to give, we just do so, knowing that we are in that instance following an inner guide, and giving what we offer to the spirit world rather than the actual individual. Some people burn incense before their shrines and altars, or place food, money, flowers or other offerings there, we elves give to the spirit by donating to the poor when the spirit moves us to do so.

It is up to each elf, however, to decide how to proceed in such matters, according to hir own conscience, hir own understanding of the Way, and what the higher spirits say to hir soul. We are not here to say everyone should be like us, or do things exactly as we do, rather that each elf will in time find hir own way and understanding of the Way, for which we provide what guidance we can that each elf will adapt to hir own needs and circumstances. Elf magic isn't necessarily about the repetition of ancient spells and formulas, although that can be pretty powerful, but first and foremost of adapting one's magic to the circumstances one encounters. If tradition works, great, if not, change it. But always understand that other elves are doing the same. That in many ways defines the Elven Way; it is the constant adaptation to changing circumstances with an eye ever on the Great Vision.

Those who are destined to be the guides and guardians of humanity and developing elven kind, the budding magical and spiritual teachers, will particularly evolve their own style of dealing with those who come to them seeking knowledge and enlightenment. Some seek healing and compassion, most hunger for personal recognition and empowerment, but the teacher often must mainly consider those lessons that will instruct the eager student in the ways to make hir progress upon the Elven Way and hir efficacy in the use of hir magic ever more successful.

This is always the teacher's first priority, to teach the lessons well. However, it should be noted that there is a transformation currently taking place between old style teachers, who were very much influenced by man, and new style teachers who are increasingly of elven kind. This is a difference between the fifth sub-race of the fifth root race and the sixth sub-race of that same race. These old style teachers can be very harsh, even brutal at times, using physical violence and condescending attitudes, much like a military boot camp, to train the student. While this may be appropriate for those training in the martial arts, it is less than effective for other studies. The new style is empowering and encouraging, helping the student to progress as much as they can to the limit of hir ability at the moment, knowing that confidence and positive reinforcement is the most effect means of conveying knowledge.

It should be noted that both these schools emphasize the importance of practice, particularly repetition of lessons, until a practical skill is mastered, combined with perseverance and endurance. The old admonition that if one doesn't succeed at first they should try and try again, endures no matter what the style of teaching.

The Elven Way

Many speak of taking the gates of heaven by storm, and there is some truth to this. The reality is that the elf, at the very beginning of hir ascent on the path of initiation, must assert hir right to make hir own choices and pursue hir own way. You cannot force the Shining Ones to help you, although they are eager to do so. Nor can you force man or others to acknowledge you, or in doing so, you are only mimicking their ways, and forcing them to vocally acknowledge what they inwardly do not feel. Rather, you must gain skill in magic and enchantment by your own right. Sometimes power can be lent to you but it is only when you have established your own power, which is to say have developed the maturity of your spirit and personality, will the world willing yield to you and the acknowledgement, for which you have so hungered, is granted without you seeking it, and often when you no longer need it. Such is the way of the world, is it not? But you cannot force your way into Faerie (or in doing so will surely regret it) any more than you can force someone to truly love you. Always, it is our own s'elves that are the key to magical power and success in all the dimensions. The way out and beyond is ever inward.

Not everyone is destined to be a king or queen of Elfin. Not everyone is destined to be a great teacher of humanity. But every spirit and soul is destined to fulfill its own nature perfectly and in doing that will attain happiness, and the recognition of the Universe and the Shining Ones in the form of magic. By this we mean that while they may not obtain worldly fame, their magical powers in their chosen field of endeavor will continually grow until they are able to perform what to less evolved individuals would appear to be miracles. These adept elven thaumaturges are a wonder for all who encounter them to behold, true masters of their chosen fields of creation.

What is most important, and among the elven adept, always the case, is that the individual receives due respect for a job well done, whatever their position, or seeming position in life, the Universe, or their society. The efficient janitor gets our respect just as much as the great novelist. This is a matter of the spirit and has little to do with the illusion of the world. A master is a master whatever hir field of endeavor. You may imagine, and you would not go far wrong, if you understood that a maid who enjoys her work cleaning hotels, could very well be a maid of the Universe in the future, cleaning up after errant spirits and setting things aright. All our skills evolve into higher and more powerful skills. Nothing we do is lost. All efforts shape our future, and all attitudes shape our character. Doing something well, shows mastery. Doing something well with style shows elven mastery. Doing something well with style and aplomb reveals the character of the elven adept.

From this we get another meaning of the axiom, As Above, So Below, or As Within, So Beyond. Our skills on a small scale of manifestation are an inkling of what we are to be. Even those things that we do that are not part of our chief ambition, like washing dishes at a restaurant to pay the rent, evolve into skills that will support our great talent. And while many folks struggle with these necessary tasks, such as working at menial tasks to support ours'elves, elves endeavor to embrace these things, enjoying and delighting in them, making them a game we play, and in so doing we master the mundane world. We weave our magic through all we do and all becomes magical down to the most mundane and material tasks.

Not only the things we do, which have a prominent effect upon the formulation of our karma and shape and reflect our future among the Shining Ones, but our personality and attitudes reflect our future as well. Some folks are extroverts and others introverts, and while this can change as we mature, often these aspects of character indicate whether we are designed to work alone in isolation, as many wizards tend to do, or with large groups, as some of the great teachers do. All that the elf will be exists within the elfin adept in the form of, as yet mostly, unrealized potentiality. The task of the Shining Ones, particularly those who deal with the development of others of their kind, is to nurture and bring forth this potentiality, helping the elf to manifest in reality, which is to say become their own true s'elf.

All these skills, however, whatever they may be, whatever ability one may have mastered, are all, beneath the surface, beneath the illusion, a mastery of magic, which is to say mastery of one's own s'elf that is the mastery of one's consciousness. The Reality of Faerie is a reality we create through consciousness by our will, guided by our intent, shaped by our vision, actualized by our beings, manifested by our bodies out of pure potential energy, which is to say the Divine Magic. It *is* eternal, and it *becomes* forever. Magic is the Source and the process for shaping that potentiality. Faerie is a work of art in progress and we are the artists. It exists in and of itself and it becomes, as we make it real, which is to say actualize it with our lives, our magic.

Unlike the world, where initiation can be given to those who are not really ready for it; where an individual can, and many often do, hold positions of authority for which they are unprepared and inadequate, in the realms of magic initiation is always achieved by real power. It is not granted, nor given, it is a natural and automatic function of one's magical attainment. This is true because Faerie, that "spiritual" world or world of spirit(s), the realms of the Shining Ones, is closer to the Divine Magic that is the Source of all things and thus purer, more direct and therefore more real than the illusionary world that most people mistake for reality.

The development of character is at the heart of elven magic, because it is a subtle and supreme power that attracts all one desires to ones'elf and becomes so potent that others aid you willing, joyfully bringing you what you desire and doing what you wish out of love and appreciation. However, this mastery, while at the heart of elven magic, is not the only mastery to be developed. Just as one need not be a good person to create great art, so one can advance in a particular skill that is useful to the Shining Ones and be incorporated into the evolution of the

Universe without the development of magical maturity. Still, without that development of character one can never reach the inner circles of magical power.

On the other hand, the Lords of Karma are not merely good spirits dedicated to maintaining balance (principally) and justice (which is really the same thing) in the Universe; they are spirits who are able to "put the smack down" on demons and other souls to be sure they receive the lessons that their behavior has magically asked for them to receive. In a sense, this is an automatic function, but there are those who service the machine, so to speak. The whole Universe is filled with Life, thus Consciousness (or in many cases Sub-consciousness).

Many spiritual books and religions speak of service, urging one to forgo one's ego and serve a higher purpose, or often just do what they tell you to do. As we've said, service is always voluntary, and in fact useless if it isn't. And while not everyone needs pursue this path of selfless service, there are those adepts who come to discover that having obtained all they wish in the world, or discovering that there is nothing of value really worth obtaining in the world, that service to others is the only thing worth doing. If you are not called to such service, and by this we mean called in your own heart, or not called as yet, you need not feel guilty about this. You may never be called. Realize that service is just another skill, like painting, like making movies, or being an accountant that the adept who is called to it may master. For some elves, their greatest talent, and this is a great skill indeed, is recognizing, nurturing and fostering the particular talents of others. We each have our place and if we follow our own desires, our true attractions and our inner feelings we will find the place, or really the path, best suited to our nature.

One seeks one's exemplars among those that inspire one. It is possible, and in fact it is frequently the case, that the particular individual whose mastery we admire might be dead, that is to say, passed on from the life where they expressed that mastery, leaving behind the masterpieces that inspire us. We can, of course, seek to contact that individual in their current life, although they may be developing other skills at this time, but usually we glean the magic they instilled in their work and which was left behind for us for that very purpose. The Shining Ones, if we are truly devoted, will see that we get those teachers, both on the material and other planes, in dreams, visions, and psychic experience, though synchronicities, which is to say the magic manifesting, that we need to further our own development. Your efforts never go unanswered, although the time frame of the Shining Ones and ours, as is so often the case with energies dealing with Faerie, may be somewhat different. Time runs differently in Faerie. It is closer to the speed of light. Ask Einstein.

> "IT IS EASY TO TRIP OVER A ROCK WHEN YOU ARE WATCHING EVERYONE ELSE'S FOOTSTEPS."
> —ELVEN WORDS TO LIVE BY

> *"It takes two to tango but only one to start a fight."*
> —*Elven Words to Remember*

> *"I am me to me and you to you,*
> *while you are me to you and you to me."*
> —*Elven Koan*
> *Note: We can see why toddlers scream on trying to learn this language. They call this the terrible twos—they got that right, you and me.)*

> *"Why Not?"*
> —*Old Elven Saying*

Brilliant they are
In every way
Light and bright
And clever we'd say
Only more than just clever
They're truly clear
That love is the magic
Most potent and dear
And with this great magic
They shelter us all
And lift us up
If ever we fall
Shining they are
The ones we adore
Who love us in turn
And will ever more
Show us the way
That to Faerie leads
Over the rocks
And through deepest weeds
Across the Earth
That is Elfin true
And among the Stars
Where wishes are too.

CHAPTER 10:
THE CHALLENGES
THAT THE ELVEN ADEPT FACES

*T*he first challenge is always this: Does one continue on the path or give up? Having awakened to one's elfin/other nature, does the elf devote hirs'elf to the Way with hir whole being or does sHe waver and perhaps abandon the way? As we've said previously, the elf is challenged, particularly in the beginning not only by strangers, and individuals certain their own path is the only true path, but even by one's friends.

This challenge, however, is presented not only at the beginning of one's awakening and shortly thereafter but can come up again and again until finally the elf is beyond being challenged in this way. When that occurs, the challenges also tend to become fewer and fewer and coincidentally others begin to respect one's devotion and give credence to one's path, even if they don't fully understand it, which without being of elfinkind is nearly impossible.

There is a particular challenge that often comes after the first year of awakening. Most basic enchantments last about a year, thus when the elf first discovers the Way, sHe is often on a type of spiritual high for that first year's time, but as the enchantment fades and the reality of still having to live within the world while pursuing the path dawns on one this reentry of the mundane into one's life can have a depressing effect on the elf. To go on after the excitement has faded, to create one's own excitement on the Way is a very real challenge that most elfin face.

You might think these challenges are about testing your

devotion to the Way, but really it's about testing your confidence in your own s'elf, for the Elven Way is flexible and is changed to the needs of each elf, but the need for s'elf confidence as a key to magical power is a permanent factor of evolutionary development whatever path one chooses to pursue. Thus one may pursue another Way, or change one's path, if they so choose, but what is important is that the individual does so on the basis of confidence in hir decisions, rather than doubt.

The next, subsequent or coincidental challenge, for it can happen later or at the same time, is the test of our ability to associate effectively with other elfin magicians. This becomes increasingly important as one ascends into the realms of the Shining Ones. Faerie is born of our loving interaction. Elfin is a love child of Elfae enchanters. By increasing our ability to weave magic collectively we extend our reach ever further and increase our powers and success thereby.

This ability to cooperate is often easier for female elves than male, this being a consequence of social evolutionary development. However, elven males in general are far better able to cooperate as equals than normal males who seem to need a strong leader to tell them what to do, or failing to have one refuse to submit to weaker authority ever vying among themselves for the position of "top dog." Therefore, in establishing an eald it is often wise to have more female than male elves, at least at first. This, however, may be different among the strongly bi or gay elves who don't suffer as much from the macho need to be on top that inflict some male elves who have been reared by normal Mankind.

Still, the tendency to jockey for position is a challenge that most have to face and it is only through time and developing magical maturity that one comes to establish cooperation, communion, and consensus as effective functioning factors in one's life and one's eald and this is true of male and female elves. The tendency to form power blocks and factions is frequent, and the adept elf must ever keep in hir mind the greater vision and empower it with hir being.

With this challenge of confronting the hunger for social position, also often comes the challenge of jealousy; this is particularly true among those Elfae who experiment with polyamoury. There is no easy answer or solution to this problem save continuing to work on ones'elf so each one becomes ever more confident in hir being, secure in hir ability to function in the world, and certain of the love and respect of hir kindred. This is a challenge that will take some time to resolve and is not a challenge just of individual elves in our current age, but one that has been going on for millennia and whose solution is still somewhat in the future of elven evolutionary development. Still, what we do now in our own lives in terms of overcoming this challenge will aid those who are yet to come, or really yet to come again (no sexual pun intended, but duly noted).

Some simply bypass this challenge in this period by returning to monogamy, which enables them to proceed with other challenges until the overall race is developed where this is less of a problem. There is nothing wrong with doing this. In fact, it is quite understandable, but the fact is in time the basis of elven association will be increasingly based on friendship, and sexual interaction will provoke no more jealousy than eating a meal together.

Those who face this particular challenge and those who temporarily bypass it are most often divided between those whose specific quest is the evolution of social morés and those who have other more pressing quests and for whom dealing with the issue of jealousy is more of an irritation and a distraction from their main quest.

As we said, multiple relationships are probably easier with one male and many females, as the Mormons have shown; but that would seldom work for elves. Elven females are unlikely to accept such a limiting and dualistic situation of double standards, and truly elven males could never convince their conscience to go along with such an unequal system.

But we should not think that this is primarily about having more sexual partners, although few elves are really opposed to that. It is about ridding our psyches of jealousy, which is a debilitating and inferior reaction that inhabits our ability to cooperate fully, become truly intimate, and arises primarily from a sense of insecurity, a lack of s'elf esteem and a fear of abandonment. The same is true of envy and other inferior characteristics that weaken the elfin enchanter.

Still, as we say, one can only deal with so much at one time and many forgo dealing with this issue directly, preferring to follow the current social fashion of serial monogamy while they concentrate on issues that seem more significant to them at this time. We do not judge either way.

And that is another challenge, which is the challenge of cooperating without relinquishing one's right as a free spirit to make one's own decisions. And on the flip side, the need to include elves into one's family, tribe, vortex, etc. without demanding that they absolutely conform to that group beyond the basic need to cooperate and relate in a loving fashion. Always, association and relationship in Faerie is voluntary in nature. If you feel a need to coerce someone into doing things in a certain way, dress according to your social mores, etc. than something is not right and the relationship will surely not last. If you are trying to organize your elf pack with the rigidity of the bureaucratic world of men and their top down dominant society, you are missing the point and losing what is precious about elven life, which is the free, creative expression of the individual in willing and joyous association with others. We can only give you a hint here, but those who gather elves need do so with a very loose grip. We must be, in a sense, like wise and loving parents who nurture and protect their children and at the same time allow them the freedom to become their own s'elves.

The Elven Way

These challenges, however, are not merely of a negative sort that is to say overcoming our shortcomings, our desires and our tendencies to anger, greed, social positioning, which is to say a hunger to be better than others, but it is also one of developing positive qualities, the most significant of these perhaps is tolerance. It is important to learn not to judge others.

Let us take for example the issue of meat eating. This is one of the primary conflicts that exist ideologically among faery kind on the material plane at this time. There are those, like these elves, who believe that vegetarianism is most likely the way elves will tend to be in the future, as we progress more and more to the place where the energy we consume will be less and less gross, until finally, having attained Divinity, which is to say unity with the Divine Magic, we will be completely s'elf existent and will need no outer sustenance at all.

In the meantime, there are elves who are vegetarian and those who still wish to eat meat. The first category sometimes looks upon the second as being un-elven, and the second insists upon their right to consume other creatures, citing it as both a natural and a historical fact of elven heredity, while some proclaim a physical need, for doing so, that it would be unhealthy for them to do otherwise. But the essence is they don't wish to be called un-elven because they eat meat.

It would be natural in this climate for some elf groups to form that are strictly vegetarian, insisting that their members don't eat meat, but it would be intolerant, in the view of these elves, to look down upon their kindred who haven't as yet (and in their own minds never will) obtain this realization. In fact, if we were part of such a vegetarian community, and we knew that certain elves snuck off now and then for a cheeseburger or a steak, we'd keep it our little secret. For us the issue isn't about vegetarianism or meat eating, it's about our own need to develop tolerance as spirits and in so doing increase the power and connection of our souls.

In point of fact, these elves, while essentially vegetarian will eat meat if we visit someone and they serve it to us. Our relationship is more important than our vegetarianism at this point. We know we are imperfect spirits, and in so knowing this of ours'elves we attempt to be much more tolerant of others.

Also, while we expect that elven communities might eat together and create only one communal meal for everyone, these elves are much more flexible. We will fix a common meal but if someone wants something different, we will fix that for them as well, or let them do so according to their own needs. Our primary goal is everyone's happiness; we have no need to make everyone conform to the group. Yes, it's sometimes a bit of extra effort, but that's what we do for those we love.

So, if you are a meat eater, we don't care. That's your business. If you don't harass us about being vegetarian or partially vegetarian, we won't bother you about eating meat. (And really in our experience meat eaters seldom bother vegetarians unless they are already feeling judged for eating meat.) The key is, as ever, developing tolerance for others as best you may and in those cases where someone's idiosyncrasies are just driving you up the wall then that is a sign from nature that you are meant to go another way. But in doing so, don't judge the person for failing to live up to your idea or ideal of what constitutes being elven, simply accept that this is an elf of a different sort. If those who pursue a particular path truly fail upon the Way, it will have ramifications in their own lives. It's nothing we really need concern ours'elves about. And if, as these elves envision, that vegetarianism is a natural development for elves upon the Way, all elves will come to it naturally, in their own time. Always, it is our own s'elves that we need be most concerned about. As we elves say, "It is easy to trip over a rock when you're spending all your time watching everyone else's footsteps."

So, too, do these elves dress as we please and expect everyone else to do likewise. It is true we frequently dress like we're in a

The Elven Way

Lord of the Rings movie, or like we teach at Hogwarts, but that's just our preference and we expect other elves will dress exactly in the fashion that calls to their hearts.

So if there is no dress code, if there is no prohibition about meat eating, is there anything that does disqualify an individual from being an elf? Only intolerance, really, and a failure to live up to their own ideals about what constitutes being elven. Each must decide for hir own s'elf what being elven means to hir and live consistently with that vision. None of us have the right to declare what being elven is for all elves, only what it is for us. Naturally, in time some behaviors and customs will fall by the wayside. Clearly those who try to tell all of us what we must be not only are losing track of the Way, but will meet the inevitable resistance that nearly all elves feel when faced with arbitrary authority. It is in our nature to make these decisions for our own s'elves and we tend to resent anyone else who tries to define us, unless it so happens we agree with them.

This much is constant. Elves ever seek the truth. Elves ever seek what is fair, both what is beautiful, elegant and magical, but what is right and just. We ever seek to increase our intelligence, to become more enlightened, for to fail to do these things, doesn't mean that one isn't elven but that one will lose touch with their elven nature in time, lose contact with Elfin itself, and fall from the Way. Elves are ever becoming. And if we are not becoming elves (principally by being elves), what are we becoming?

So we do not judge. One is either developing one's own s'elf as best sHe may, becoming ever more and greater, increasing hir talents, skills, abilities and magic, or one isn't doing so, and our opinions on this matter are of little relevance. Even the Shining Ones don't really judge. It's a function of Nature. You are or you aren't and it's ever and always totally up to you. Beside, one may stray and return again. It wouldn't be the first time it's happened. We've been there. Most elves have. If you are doing your best that is certainly good enough for us, and good enough for the Shining Ones.

So that is the real challenge, the day-to-day challenge of persevering or not. In the end, only true elves will endure on this path and that is a truth of the Elven Way. And remember, in the end it is not your failures that will be counted up, but your successes, the quests you have mastered, the abilities you've developed, the amazing things you have created, the kindred you have helped upon the way. The rest is just a bit of drama in the Universal play. Karma is transitory; enlightenment is eternal.

And here's another challenge. A particularly elven challenge of making it all, in as much as possible, something we enjoy even when we struggle to do it. We love being elves and that love spreads into the whole of our lives touching everything and everyone we encounter. Coming to enjoy the process takes true mastery. Sometimes, we must struggle to enjoy it. It doesn't come without effort, but as we put in more and more effort the easier it becomes, and turning it into delight makes it easier yet. It is an elf trick and not immediately mastered, but for those who understand, it helps to make the all of life go a little smoother. What is life in Faerie like? It's what you make it. And what would you make of Faerie? What would you create with your magical power? That is the all-important question, for you are creating your own Eald, your own dimension of Faerie with every thing you think and do.

So how does the elf balance being and becoming? One needs to learn from others, from Masters, from other traditions, and humble ones'elf enough to do so, and at the same time one needs to become increasingly s'elf aware, confident in one's own Elfhood, and reserve the right to think for one's s'elf and make one's own decisions. The Path is a tightrope that one must continually walk in which one gives credit where credit is due to those that have been one's benefactors, and at the same time increase the potency of one's own vision and understanding. For elves, our path is increasingly eclectic. We pick and chose from other spiritual and magical traditions, our own for the most part having been obscured by the fantasies of those who do not know, or destroyed by the dominators who ever insist that their way is the only way, their god the one true god, and they are always right, and even if they aren't they have the power, so suck on it.

You have to trust your own heart, your own instincts and feelings. There is no other way. Naturally, as we rise upon the path we receive help and guidance from others, but in many ways this is like having people telling you what movies or books they really like. You may or may not react to them or enjoy them, or get from them what they did, or be moved as they were moved by them. Faerie calls to each of us in the way that speaks to our own soul. We are all journeying to Faerie, but the journey for each of us is different, our path unique while at the same time being similar to others. It's like traveling down a road from one town to another, even if we take the same road we don't necessarily see the same things as we pass by, and there is in fact more than one way to get from here to there.

And how does one remain humble in the face of enlightenment and at the same time develop the confidence to begin to chart one's own course and path? How can one be humble and equal at the same time? Actually, that part is rather simple. Modesty is a magic that produces many benefits. If we give praise generously to others, while remaining modest about our own talents and abilities, Nature itself, which ever seeks balance, will see that we get due credit in time. By being respectful of all spirits, both those above us and those below, we become accepted as equals by all enlightened spirits. By acknowledging that there are those who are smarter than us, more beautiful, more successful in the world, more knowledgeable, more skilled at this or that or the other thing, while being true to our own unique s'elf and doing all we can to improve ours'elves, we give each their due without envy and we find what we most wish in the first place, which is the path to success for our own s'elves; optimizing thereby every opportunity and in this way increasing our luck and our magic.

The Elven Way like all paths requires effort, but it does not have to be hard, though life often is, it does not have to involve suffering, though karma sometimes does. The Elven Way is a path designed to soothe the hard and make it easier, to heal the suffering by eliminating the roots of suffering, which is to say karma, and to promote increasing success, and thus confidence, for our own true s'elves as we empower all our others.

All the while, these challenges and struggles that we encounter are for the most part, if we are truly adept, unseen by the outside world. Most of what we encounter, most of the effort, most of our magic, goes on within us and is never noted by those who rush by us in the world. Although in fact, for some of these folks a person could be on fire and they still wouldn't notice.

And the more and more adept we become the less and less do these struggles affect the outside world. In this way we transform ours'elves, cutting the cords of karma that bind, transforming suffering through inner endurance and sacrifice, standing in the long line of the pecking order and not passing on the stings to which we have been subjected. No easy task this, but we have our kindred always, the Shining Ones, the power of Faerie, ever sending us magic to uplift us. They know; they have been there thems'elves; they have endured the challenges we face and overcome them. They, with unending compassion, donate regularly to the fund for the victims of living in the Kala Yuga, the dark ages of evolution, or as it is more commonly called: the modern world.

As we endure and overcome these challenges, and in the course of doing so begin to enjoy the challenge, and even as we are supported in our efforts by our kindred who are also on the path and the Shining Ones who are farther on the path than we are currently, we gradually develop increasing independence, resilience and s'elf reliance. We are becoming ever more elven, which is to say, increasingly in touch with our Divine nature,

The Elven Way

the Magic that abides ever within us. More and more we progress to the place where we don't need others, yet paradoxically, for elves at least, this is the level where we become increasingly adept at cooperating with others. We could create our own worlds, totally independent of others; we could create our own Universe. But our souls delight in each other. Our spirits delight in variety and we increasingly become open to more and more creative spirits. The deeper we go into Faerie the more we confront the paradoxes of Elfin life and in confronting them embrace them, and in embracing them merge them like lovers who are One and Separate at the same time. This is Elven Alchemy.

Those sorcerers, who seek power for their selves alone will end up alone together, like starved and ravenous rats locked with each other in a cage. They will eat each other until only one is left and that one will starve. This comes from ever taking more than one gives, increasing the parasitic principle within ones'elf. We elves ever seek to create balance, always give back to those who have benefited us and if we can, give them even more, although sometimes what they give and what we gift to them are different. They may buy us dinner; we may repay them with joyous and faithful loyalty, or vice versa. This is not an exact balance but a flowing one. We are not, or most of us aren't, accountants (We know some elves who are. It's a good way to pass through the world.). We don't keep track in exact detail everything we've done for others, but we remember all they have done for us and ever send them blessings in return. This is what we receive from the Shining Ones, blessings eternal that we may transform into magic by which we may change the world.

They know what we are going through. They know that we can make use of their assistance and they give it willingly. They see thems'elves in us, born anew in a unique way and know that in empowering our magic that our eventual creativity will repay them with beauty and wonder. So do we return their kindness in helping others on the Way for the Shining Ones are passing to us what was given to them so we might further pass it on to those coming after us. Inspiration is a magic that continually increases in power. A poem inspires a poet who creates another poem that inspires another poet, and so on, its power growing with every creation. So are we poems, unique creative expressions of the Magic, born of our own will to be, magic come to life in our being. Where does this end? It doesn't. We create eternally becoming ever more and greater.

> "Simplifying one's life is like doing dishes, even when you've washed them all they're never done."
> —Old Elven Saying

The Elven Way

THE DAWN COMES
ON A BRIGHT ELVEN DAY
AND ONCE AGAIN
WE FOLLOW THE WAY
PURSUING THE LIGHT
THAT STARS TO US GIVE
SO WHATEVER LIFE BRINGS
THE WAY WE DO LIVE
THE WAY OF THE ELVEN
THE WAY OF THE FAIR
THE WAY OF THOSE FAE
WHO EVER DO CARE
NO MATTER WHAT COMES
WHAT PROBLEMS DO RISE
TOGETHER WE TRAVEL
ON THE PATH OF THE WISE
WHAT CHALLENGE MAY LOOM
WE EAGER EMBRACE
FOR THAT IS THE WAY
OF THE BRIGHT ELVEN RACE.

CHAPTER 11:
RELATING TO THE SHINING ONES

As we've said, our relationship with the Shining Ones is, in essence, one of family. It is intimate as deep friendship can be intimate. It is frasority (combining the words for fraternity and sorority), a brother/sisterhood of kindreth dedicated to the illumination of the world, the empowerment of individual spirits and the fulfillment of each one's soulful longings. It is natural in formation, de fact in its existence thus it is esoteric. It is an inner frasority rather than an exoteric organization.

It is only natural that individuals will attempt to create this frasority exoterically, that is to say create churches, lodges, temples and fellowships in imitation of the true frasority. After all, we are here to merge the material and spiritual worlds, to bring illumination, thus magic into the world. However, know that it is extremely unlikely that most organizations would even come close to representing the true frasority, although again that doesn't mean they shouldn't try to do so. And it is surely possible, even likely, that adepts from the true esoteric frasority will be members of one or more of these exoteric hierarchies. It is, however, just as likely, or unlikely in this case, that all the members will be true adepts, or that the hierarchy of the organization will truly reflect the spiritual development and level of adeptship of its members.

And while these things are extremely unlikely, at the same time it is nigh on impossible that there will be one organization, as opposed to any others, that has true adepts exclusive to any others. However, it is near inevitable at this point in evolution that you will encounter some organization that will make such a claim to exclusivity.

Here we come to the idea of the bloodline, the genetic, cultural, ethnic, educational and social inheritance that denotes that one is an elf, a fae, or/and also an adept. This material line of descent, while having some small validity, that is to say, education, breeding, and genes are not without their effect upon the individual. They are however no guarantee of adeptship nor are those who lack the particularly ascribed genes barred from the true frasority.

No one can bar any spirit from joining or advancing within the realms of Faerie adeptship. Not race, religion, genetic background, financial or social status or anything else bars one from enlightenment and thus from the acquisition of magical power, although some of these things can make its attainment more difficult. Know that in every race there are those who are descended from the faerie folk, and every spirit whatsoever has a right to pursue the Elven Way. This is a path of spirit, which means action combined with sincere intent. Only the individual hir own s'elf can decide ultimately to join the esoteric frasority, and sHe does so by the pursuit of truth and elevation of hir spirit, soul and hir others. Only the individual spirit can prevent hir own entry into Faerie by actions that are counter to the Way and thus impede hir progress on the path to Faerie.

The only thing that those who would deny others their right to pursue the path will accomplish is a karmic responsibility that will most likely manifest in such a way as to compel them to be born within the race, or ethnic group that the individual attempted to impede.

It is true that for those who are insecure, such claims to exclusive adeptship, the true and only bloodline, etc. are a temporary salve for their wounded ego. And, honestly, we have compassion for their struggles. But we must tell them, or we don't have to do so (but fair warning is only fair, yes?), that in seeking to bar others they are only really managing to obstruct their own souls and impede their own progress, and we for our part are loath to have them do that. Though they are not yet ready, they are always welcome to join us when they can give up their hunger to be more important than others and join our kindred in this great quest as the equals we recognize them to be.

The true frasority is based exclusively on merit. One has either chosen to join or not, and one has either achieved a certain level or adeptship or not. For our own part, we are eager to have you among us. The Elven Way is less about altars and more about alters, the true transformation and transubstantiation of the soulful spirit. (For a more extensive explanation of the soul and spirit see our book *Through the Mists of Faerie*.)

All that those who create a particular exoteric system of esoteric study are really doing is beginning to create a particular strain of elves, or a school of adeptship. This does not mean that others can't be elves or adepts, but that others are not of that particular lineage. So, too, it is that in formulating our Elven Way we are offering certain paths toward Mastery, Illumination and Power. But that does not mean these are the only paths, and individuals can be adepts without being elven or faerie adepts. Of course, in point of fact, one doesn't have to an elf or a fae to pursue the Elven Way anymore than one has to be an American to drive from Miami to Washington, D.C., or has to be a citizen of Singapore to fly on Singapore airlines. The way to adeptship and the true frasority is open to every spirit. We are just a small part of a vast reality.

Choosing a Master

While the Way is one of increasing s'elf confidence and cooperative independence, one has to learn from someone. It goes nearly without saying that when one begins one feels uncertain and confused. The way is open before one, filled with possibilities but the beginner seldom knows what to do next and naturally looks to those more experienced to guide hir.

Especially, sHe looks to hir inner guides, the spirits who speak to us in dreams and intuitions and who act through synchronicities to give us some hint at the direction to go in. It is true that there are those who seem to awaken who already have some sense of their elven nature, but these have already progressed on the Way in previous lifetimes and are just re-awakening and taking up the quest, usually after the recapitulation of their previous lives that tends to occur in their first 28 to 30 years of age, that is to say prior to their first Saturn Return. Exoterically, they appear to be beginners, but esoterically they are not.

Exoterically, as well we can choose a Master or a teacher/guru to guide us, but esoterically the Master, or Masters who come to us are those with whom we've already developed relationships in previous lifetimes. We may have been the dog, cat or other *pet* of a Shining One; we probably have been this Shining One's apprentice in many lifetimes and, in a sense, still are. It is possible that a whole new relationship will form with a new Master, but that is extremely rare. We have formed links and bonds of magic, obligation and connection lifetime after lifetime and those who are already, in a very real sense, our magical family, tend to look out for us. From this comes the popular idea of the personal guardian angel.

Naturally, as we advance on the path and tend therefore to individuate and explore various specialties, we also come under the guidance or in contact with those who work in the same areas. This relationship however develops naturally, out of attraction. In this case, it is the attraction that exists between those who share a profound interest.

So unlike the exoteric world where you choose the college of your choice, and if accepted pay the fees, and get whatever teachers they may have, the esoteric schools (and by here we don't mean exoteric schools that teach esoteric subjects but the actual inner schools) are composed of those who are instinctually, as well as karmically, drawn together.

How then does one choose or find a teacher/Master? One does so quite simply by hanging out in the world with those to whom one is attracted and pursuing one's chosen fields of endeavor and study. One's Masters will be there awaiting one.

For most folks their choice of religious belief helps determine the Master they get. Christians get certain masters, Moslems get masters that specialize in that faith. Pagans get the masters dealing with the particular gods or goddesses to whom they pay homage. We should not think by this, however, that these masters have the same rivalry that the devotees of those faiths sometimes have concerning each other. On the higher levels the masters are aware that the esoteric family is one and all seeming conflicts on the mundane plane are a function of ignorance and misunderstanding concerning the true nature of reality. What masters do Atheists get, you might ask? Usually those involved in promoting various sciences. Of course, atheists don't believe there are such things as invisible masters, but that doesn't mean they don't receive care and guidance, they just don't perceive, or acknowledge, its esoteric nature.

Astrological and Other Influences Of Attraction

There are also spirits and masters, Shining Ones, who are attached to us due to the astrological influences under which we are born, according to the day we were born upon and so on. Those who think that our birth is somehow arbitrary are mistaken. We are born when we are according to the working out of our karma and our destiny. Our destiny, remember, is ultimately always to become enlightened and to fulfill ours'elves perfectly as individual soulful spirits. The astrological chart doesn't force us, as some believe, to be one way or another, but rather is a generalized description of the solar influences surrounding this particular incarnation. It doesn't really force us to do or be anything in particular, rather it tends to note the opportunities and restrictions we will probably face in our life, as well as the tools, particularly those of personality and character that will be available to us for dealing with those things.

Naturally, while the path itself remains the same in its cosmic scope, the masters differ in their natures. Remember, the more advanced we become the more unique and individual we become. They each have their particular idiosyncrasies, and in fact, it is these aspects of personality that tend to attract us to one rather than another. Thus also the way they teach is also often unique. There is no one right way, except the way that works to further you on the path.

Understand that in taking you on as a pupil the master is, in part, assuming responsibility for you. It is not that the master will be punished if you make a mistake, but what parent doesn't ache to see their beloved child err? Also, you should note that your master's own elevation depends in part on your success. If you don't rise to take hir place, sHe can't relinquish it.

However, the Shining Ones have bodies that are more ethereal than ours and thus function in our dimension from a kind of distance, therefore we are also often in need of more immediate masters/teachers/gurus/guides who are currently incarnated as we are. Some of these are Shining Ones functioning as bodhisattvas, that is enduring this world for our benefit, but there are others who, like we, must work out their own karma as well as work through the various limitations that come from being born into a particular cultural, ethnic, racial (both mundane and spiritual race), and social upbringing with its tendencies toward skewing our perceptions. Of course, what makes them masters is that they tend to work through these limitations very quickly and rise in short time to a more cosmic, spiritual and universal understanding of life.

While one can deal with those who are masters of a particular art or science, who can be great at what they do but not necessarily great or even likable people, the esoteric masters of the path of light are all morally developed individuals (unless, of course, they follow the path of dominance and wickedness that seeks to enslave rather than liberate spirits). This does not mean that they strictly follow the proscribed laws and morés of a particular culture, but that they know and follow the dictates of what is fair and just in a universal sense and act in regards to the well being, healing and enlightenment of all they encounter. While this moral development is not necessary in a worldly sense, and certainly not required among those sorcerers following the path of dominance who seek power over others, it is absolutely vital among those who wish to ascend to the realms of the Shining Ones, the inner reaches of Elfin.

Naturally, those masters who are closer to us on the path and just above us in evolutionary development also have to go through the recapitulation period of the first Saturn Return, and it is usually not until after that that they truly begin to manifest their powers fully and to take up the training of others. Of course, there are exceptions to this, as with all things, and this is not a rule but a tendency of the way things are prone to occur. It is in part because of this that wisdom is often associated with age.

It is thus that we find human beings who are great geniuses or seeming saints who dedicate their lives to helping those in the world, which after all is what they have come here to do, who none the less turn out to be imperfect souls. Being dedicated as they are, one might even say in a way obsessed with the task at hand, they sometimes don't bother to work on the various aspects of personality that would make them more pleasant to be around and that would in many ways help serve their own spirit. Their only interest at this point is in helping out on the material plane, or accomplishing a particular quest they have undertaken, and they have set aside personal gain to do so. Of course, in fact, this effort will lead to the expansion of their soulful nature, even while some, perhaps many folks will find them to be a bit prickly.

We elves, however, are most often enchanters, and the development of the personality is a primary effort and is part and parcel of every other quest we pursue. While that makes us less likely to abandon the development of our personality to pursue other skills or devote ours'elves purely to service, it does help us to be more tolerant and able to deal with those who do. Thus we often serve as the chosen assistants for those sorts of Masters, since few others can stand being around these obsessed individuals for too long. We not only soothe them, but also soothe others who encounter them.

On the other hand, while our Master Teachers, or teachers of mastery really, look for us and guide us as best they can, there are limitations concerning how much they can do for us. This may in part be a limitation of their power, for they are not all powerful, although a great deal more powerful than we, but it can also be a limitation imposed by the principles that guide them concerning us. They cannot really interfere with our karma and if they shield us too much we may turn out weak when we need to be strong. After all, the whole point is to nurture and foster our independence as spirits, not make us eternally dependent on them.

However, least we become too self-centered, as many seem to be when thinking they have a guardian angel specifically assigned to eternally watch over them, most Masters are multi-taskers. They guide us, while developing their own souls and spirits as they dedicate thems'elves to the process of creating their own particular vision. As we say, the higher you go, the more eccentric it gets. It is likely, however, that the master or masters you get will be in many ways similar in disposition to the inclinations of your own spirit, even if it vexes you when encountering them. They are the grindstone, we the magical blade being sharpened.

Two forces come into effect in this. The first is Like Attracts Like. As we said, we are endlessly attracted to others who are interested in the same things we are. This is an essential but not

The Elven Way

all encompassing tendency, which is balanced by the force of Opposites Attract. While we pursue those influences that attract us as spirits, there is also a part of our own spirit that wishes us to be ever stronger, and thus to overcome every weakness. The Universe, also, functioning through our soul seeks to bring us into continual balance. Thus, while we tend to encounter masters who pursue the same studies that appeal to us, we also draw to us those masters, who are in many ways our opposite, and thus will try our souls, to challenge us to bring balance to our spirits and to master any weakness we may have.

Naturally, most of us tend to prefer the first type of master over the second, but that is the point of the realms of magical initiation. The second master ever promotes adaptability, flexibility and an expansion of our soulful connections while helping us to rid ours'elves of prejudice, preconception and a tendency to narrow ours'elves at the expense of our magical power. Whatever we lack in our quest for mastery, they will discover and challenge us to obtain and acquire through persistent effort and devotion. It is like someone who hates math having to go to advanced algebra. As we develop as masters, ours'elves, we learn to accept and embrace these challenges, making them easier on us. As we give up our resistance and join the flow, the Way becomes so much easier.

However, as we point out, this is only part of getting one's Masters degree in the esoteric school of Life. And it is really for our own benefit and these courses are required by our own higher s'elf, which is to say our own longing to become greater and more powerful. And these courses are balanced by all the wondrous electives we get to choose and study because they teach us the subjects we love and are most interested in.

Excuse us if we use a lot of educational analogies, but this is what we know from our own path, but if truth be told and we are determined to do so, there is also a tendency for the higher magics to attract individuals who have at least a college degree, although that is in no way required. The only things required are devotion to develop one's spirit with an unstinting will combined by a compassionate understanding of humanity and of life in general, and a resolve to do what is fair and right for all concerned ever with an eye toward the enlightenment, empowerment and realization of every soulful spirit. We're not asking much of ours'elves are we?

As we've expressed, the taking on of a pupil by the master is both an act of compassion, and of s'elf interest. Compassion because often the master's work doesn't need pupils to be fulfilled, although having apprentices can be helpful, even though their work at first tends of necessity to be inadequate, and eventually the pupil becomes a master, which rebounds to the master's own benefit, glory and positive karma. It is a win-win situation, but not an absolutely required one. Again, participation on almost every level is voluntary.

Thus we owe the master a real debt that we repay by doing our best, honoring those who have been our benefactors and, as humbly as we can, fulfilling the challenges they set before us for our own good; and further we honor them by helping others who come to us seeking help, guidance and our sagely advice, such as it is.

"Elven magic isn't so much about altars, but alters."
—Old Elven Knowledge

If you ask the elves if everyone has a bit of elf in them, they will answer: "If they wish!"
—What Elves Say

"What does it take to tread the Elven Way? Everything you have. All of your heart, all of your soul, and all that you do every night and day."
—Elven Words to Live By

The Elven Way

They write of Elven Kingdoms
And Elvish Queendoms, too
And clans and mobs
And bands that throb
And all of this we do
But most of all we're family
From littlest to big
From wee folk
To the very great
In shiny velvet rig
And in that magic family
Love does ever reign
Not queen, nor king or mighty chief
But affection never fain
For friendship ever rules us
And loyalty sincere
And most of all abiding love
For all whom we hold dear.

CHAPTER 12:
MORE ON THE ELVEN STAR AND THE RAYS OF MANIFESTATION

The first three rays are often called the primary rays and are related to the primary colors, red, yellow and blue. The fourth and other three rays are secondary rays, although the fourth is separate from the last three, being, in a sense a negotiating ray, or arbitrating ray and is related to black, white, thus gray and silver, and the rainbow. The fifth, sixth, and seventh ray reflect the secondary colors of orange, green and purple. However, don't let this differentiation fool you. Each ray has an aspect of the others in it. No one reflects absolutely one without another and the colors stem from the same source and are only separate as a device for thinking about them, just as the all of Life is One, but differentiates for the beauty of manifestation.

The three primary rays guide the course of evolution. The first reveals the Vision and is the Master of the Elemental forces, by which we mean the pure undifferentiated energy that composes all things and outlines its materialization on various levels and dimensions. This Master is related to the first ray and may be called the Writer or the Architect.

The second Master is the Master of Love and ensures that a spark of the Divine exists in all things, by which we mean the urge toward success and perfection exists in all that manifests. All life seeks its Divine Realization. It strives toward happiness and the fulfillment of the soul and ensures balance in the Universe and continuity of the Plan. This Master is sometimes called the Producer, for it brings or binds everything together and is related to the second ray.

The third is the Master of Individuation and Initiation and oversees that all things are unique unto thems'elves and fulfill thems'elves perfectly. This Master is the Master of the five other rays, and teaches the magical powers that each needs to find and know its true s'elf. We might call this one the Director for sHe gives direction to those who seek to help fulfill the Vision, sets them to their particular tasks and helps them obtain the skills they need to do so. (Note: some might switch the aspects of the first and third ray, making the third the writer or philosopher, and the first the director. We leave it to you to decide which way you wish to view it. Remember that what we offer here is merely a formulation of the truth, the absolute truth being beyond any intellectual theorizing.)

We could relate these to the aspects of the Divine trinity of Hindu mythology Creation, Maintenance, and Destruction or Dissolution, but only imperfectly. The first ray pronounces the Vision, the second maintains it by linking all things together, but the third keeps all things in motion though creative individualization. We could look at it, for our own part, like making a movie. The writer gives us the script, and the producer gets the people together to make the film, but the director, the actors, the set designers all put in their own creative influence as they fulfill their part under the director's guidance as sHe interprets the writer's vision. What eventuates is a cooperative creative project. So also do we carry out the Vision of the great Shining Ones, who give us the major themes of the Vision, draw us together in the project, that is to say our particular dimension, while we under their guidance (the laws and rules of karma) creatively fulfill our part.

From these first three rays, the seven rays are born and delineate the major areas of power and development in the Universe and our particular dimension of manifestation. However, due to personal creative input, different individuals relate, as we said previously, to one or two rays more than others. We might call these their primary rays. Those who have 1st ray predominating, for instance, often tend toward exploring, inspiring, and being leaders. In this case we mean leaders as in pioneers and explorers more then we mean arbitrary authorities or officials. The writer is the creative mind that inspires the project, or movie, etc. but there are also individuals who are the head of costume design, scenery, and so forth, sub-heads that seek to bring to life the writer's vision.

Also, the different rays manifest their power more in some realms than others. The 1st, 4th, and 7th rays are very materially oriented, while the 2nd and 6th rays have their greatest power and influence, as well as interest, on the astral planes of feeling, desire and relationship/connection/communion, and the 3rd and 5th are strongest on the mental planes of manifestation, the world of ideas, thoughts and ideals.

They each have their challenges. Those of the 1st, 4th, and $7^{th,}$ rays, which are very concerned with mastering manifestation on the mundane plane, deal with the challenges of that dimension, which can include a denseness and a slowing of time, as well as the obstacles one faces when confronted with making real the first ray visionary's design. While those of the 2nd and 6th rays, which deal with the astral planes, have to encounter raging desires and emotions and bring these into balance and channel them toward the desired end. The emotional trauma drama of the world is their orbit of mastery. And the 3rd and 5th adepts are engaged primarily in mastering their mental capacities, and bringing to rein the wild and unruly mind.

Again, while these seem separate, it is clear to the adept that these are coordinated efforts, the mastery of one of which furthers the mastery of others, but by no means eliminates that need. Always the goal is complete and balanced fulfillment of one's potentiality. It is not a question of brains over brawn, but of developing brains and brawn, along with social, emotion maturity and integrity of action and intent. The wimpy nerd will develop their body and their social acumen, while the muscular but intellectually challenged athlete will develop hir minds as well as hir body.

Those who follow the first ray are particularly influenced to develop charismatic power in addition to becoming a shining example of magical potential. These individuals are the inspiration for the development of fashion, social morés, and particular aspects of a developing race of evolving being and as they advance are able to draw down the energy from the stars to aid with this activity. They are star enchanters of a high order, singularities whose unique way of being is idolized and followed by other spirits seeking their own path as they diverge from the mass of humanity. Because of the significance of their activity, the proclamation of the Vision with their very lives, it becomes increasingly important that they are shining examples of certain primary aspects to be developed by evolving humanity (or whoever they are an example for) such as courage, daring, fortitude, integrity, and honor.

Also, these must develop a certain disinterest in the opinions of the mass of humanity. They must pursue their course regardless of the criticism they may encounter via peer pressure and social scorn from those around them. They must demonstrate that they are stronger and more resilient than the mass of public opinion. At the same time, these bear a responsibility to choose a way that leads to the improvement of the race, so while it may seem that they are totally isolated from most of humanity, they are in fact acting for its benefit, seeking by their actions to set it free and setting the example for others that will follow their lead. They are the alpha mutation. Naturally, those who come after them will explore further, establish other paths from the main path that the first ray singularity blazed, and this is what they are meant to do. So it is that we elves tell you that in following the Elven Way, you must think and decide for your own s'elf what is right for you, what works for you, and expect that in doing that you will let your inspiration create even more of our beautiful and wondrous culture.

You have probably met one of two of these charismatic beings, utterly confident and without doubt about what they are doing. They inspire people, and people submit to them willingly, doing

The Elven Way

things they'd never think of doing otherwise and you might wonder, how did they get them to do that? The answer is first ray magic. They're nearly fearless, or seem so, blazing a trail through the world as though it is the wide-open wilderness, which for them it is. They are like an artist that has been dropped into a studio full of canvas and paint. They just go for it. The world is a blank slate, a blank canvas, a blank sheet of paper and they fill it full of their vision and when they do, you see it too, awakening your imagination, so you can't help but step into that world, and what is more, you hunger to do so. They bring fantasy alive, they bring Faerie alive; this is elven magic.

There are many that aspire to this power. But few who are at this point ready to achieve it. Many, many try and fail. But don't let that put you off if you are one of these. Your aspiration is your destiny. Keep trying and you will develop the skills and powers needed. But remember, this requires all of what you have and are. It is not a power easily achieved and you must strive endlessly, continually transforming yours'elf, improving yours'elf until the lifetime arrives when effort falls away and action takes hold. Which is not to say you will be totally perfected, few such first ray adepts are, but you will be a wonder none-the-less and what foibles you have will only serve to make you more approachable, to keep you in touch with those you are meant to serve and guide.

The 2nd ray adepts are quite different from the 1st ray adepts. These are the lords and ladies of compassion. Compared to them the 1st ray adepts can seem totally heartless at times, focused on the goal and nothing else. But the 2nd ray adepts are focused on people, on their welfare, their problems, and these tend to have almost nothing in the way of what most folks refer to as ego. They are near completely focused on others. These are the servers, the Mother Theresa-s, the Gandhi-s, the Dalai Lamas (although both Mother Theresa and Gandhi also had very strong 1st and 3rd ray aspects), who seek in all ways to bring healing and understanding to the world and to aid each and all to cooperate for mutual benefit. These are your great Healers. Here are your Earth Mother types who take care of the whole family, tribe, clan, vortex, and so on. Their joy comes from nurturing others. They encourage mutual understanding and cooperation, bring together those who can work together, or whose talents will produce something amazing, and they are an effective and necessary balance to the 1st ray adepts. The 1st ray adepts are often out there, out in space, bringing in and actualizing through their lives visions of the future, while the 2nd ray adepts begin to make it practically realizable by encouraging those who can manifest it.

However, it is the 3rd ray adepts who shall take the vision of the 1st ray, and the gathered clan that the 1st ray attracts but the 2nd ray holds together, and turns these into a working plan. In many ways, the 3rd ray adepts translate the vision of the 1st ray adepts, so the group the 2nd ray has united, nurtured and feed, will understand their part in the plan in a practical way. The 1st ray adept says this is the way it can be, opening the realms before them. The 2nd assures them they can do it and encourages them to do so, while the third tells them in realistic terms how it can be done.

The realm of the 3rd ray adept is knowledge and while that still is generalized in a sense, for it will be further delineated by 5th ray technicians, the 3rd ray gives increased direction, illuminating hir own understanding of the 1st ray vision, and how it can be achieved.

These rays are often paired, the 1st ray with the 7th, the 2nd ray with the 6th, and the 3rd with the 5th, with the 4th ray balancing all of them or creatively filling in, which is to say if a 1st ray needs a 7th ray assistant but one isn't available a 4th ray adept will take on the aspect of a 7th ray temporarily. But in a way you could also say that the 5th ray is born of the interaction of the 1st and 2nd rays, the 6th arises from the merging of the 2nd and 3rd rays, and the 7th from the blended aspects of the 3rd and 1st. Again, the 4th stands alone in a sense or combines all of them at once. It is a sort of catch all of creative endeavor and serves as a moderating force between all the others. The 4th accepts all while proclaiming the right for each to pursue its own direction. As we said it is black and white, thus all the gray tones between, or silver, but it is also brown, which is what one gets when one blends all the colors together. It is particularly important during transition periods when one race begins to emerge from another, or when a new sub-race develops from the root race, which is occurring at the time of this writing. Elves are generally very comfortable in the eclectic, catch all 4th ray environment.

The 5th ray individuals tend to be technicians. They are experts at various fields of endeavor. They are scientists, but mostly they take general knowledge, abstract knowledge, and turn it into practical knowledge that can make things happen in the world. They are often your Jack-of-All-Trades, your jerry rigging masters of making it happen. You tell them what you need done, they figure out how to do it. These are often elven Rangers, able to fit in and find a job anywhere, although they have a restless spirit and often bounce from job to job.

6th ray individuals are devoted servers. They may not have a particular expertise, but they are willing to help out wherever they can and know that there is always something for a willing extra pair of hands to do. They are the acolytes of elven magic. Whatever is needed they will do if they can, eager to bring the magic to fruition. They believe in the vision and they want to see it fulfilled and because of their adaptable natures they work easily together. These will learn any and every job and in time rise to function in one of the primary rays if needed although their aspiration really is just to be of help. They are idealistic and drawn by the Vision of the 1st ray enchanters and the 3rd ray magicians who seek to fulfill it.

Ceremonial magic and ritual is the province of the 7th ray adepts, who are masters of orderliness. They know that routine helps create efficiency and seek to streamline all things to their most effective function. They organize storage. They keep lists of tools that are needed and where they are kept. They make sure that all things flow smoothly in a consistent fashion. If you need it, they know where to find it. They are the bureaucrats of the Universe. And they are the ones that keep the ancient lore, knowing that in tradition and repetition there is power.

As we've said these are just generalized descriptions of the rays and no one individual is composed of any one ray, we all have all the rays within us. However, certain individuals have some rays more pronounced in their being than others and this is in part due to the process of individuation that helps give the world its variety and beauty. It should not be felt that being one ray is better than being another, except in so much as it is the best ray for you at this time. All have contributions they make to the whole and without each of them we would be very much deprived.

Also, it would be a mistake to think that an elf is composed primarily of one or more ray(s) forever. Different lifetimes see us accepting different challenges and thus working within some rays more than others for that purpose. It is true that if you very much admire the efforts and activity of a particular ray, or are greatly drawn to it, then you are destined to undertake the esoteric and exoteric course of study that develops those facilities and when your time comes will manifest your skills for the benefit of all.

The important thing always is to do your best with what you have in the area you are currently studying. Most modern people think of the world in terms of success or failure, rewards or punishment. Certainly, karma is most often viewed as punishment for previous lifetimes. But we are not assigned to a particular ray to punish us. The masters do not punish us. The challenges we face are a direct consequence of the magic we have done. Karma is an exact reaction to our activities in previous lifetimes. But this isn't punishment, although it can surely seem so, but is automatic function of our magic. These are the lessons we have undertaken, the challenges we require of ours'elves evoked by our own actions. Some outside force, god or person is not punishing us; we are engaged in the evolutionary path we have chosen, by action, which is to say magic, which is activated by the deeds we have done.

The rays are like threads with which we can weave a wondrous tapestry of life. We can make it into a magic carpet that will sail us into the future we envision. They come from the light of the Universe, separated by the prism of our individuality, creating a rainbow of possibilities.

Understand that these functions extend outward. On earth we may write a novel or create a movie. Later, we create the matrix of social thought and philosophy. Later still we create planets and deal with developing races upon them, as we increasingly refine, expand and develop our various talents, powers and abilities. Thus will we create our own eald. Thus Faerie was created. It exists in pure potentiality, but it is ever we who must make it manifest in reality.

And in saying this we don't mean simply creating a place we call Faerie or Elfin. That is to say building a city or a country we call Elven, which is what the 1st, 4th and 7th rays primarily do. It is also about creating the feeling and ambience of Faerie, the feeling of magic and love, joy and happiness, and cooperative and healing interaction, the function of the 2nd, 4th and 6th rays. And further it is the development of the philosophies of Faerie, the techniques of Elfin magic, the increasing power over one's mind and consciousness, the providence of the 3rd and 5th rays. All these together are needed, both for the elf as an individual and for elves as a community, a people. Just as the seven-pointed star, the elf star is one, so are the rays one magic manifested in various ways.

The rays are light, the rays are magical power; the rays are the means we have to get what we desire in the Universe. Reach out now and gently take hold of a thread of light and begin to tug ever so carefully, pulling what you desire toward you. Now shape it into a vision you have in mind of what you will to be. So shall you weave your future.

> "Even the rocks stand in their way."
> —An Old Elven Saying, meaning the All of Nature opposes it

> "We elves tend to be very traditional and conservative in a very radical and liberal way."

Oh! Elven Star most wondrous
Ye of seven points
Bright your light
Within our sight
That in our soul anoints
Every bit of magic
Every wish and spell
Every deep enchantment
Blessed by sacred well
Flowing forth into the world
And blessing all it finds
Waking Faerie in the soul
And every heart and mind
Arousing spirit joyous
Alive with courage great
Ready to encounter life
And solve the great debate
Who are we?
We are the star
Manifest and true
Being our own elfin s'elves
What else is there to do?

CHAPTER 13:
REQUIREMENTS FOR ELVEN ADEPTSHIP AND MASTERY

So who can tread this path of elven magic? Anyone who desires to do so and supports that aspiration with energy; which is to say action; which is to say magic. It doesn't matter where you are now, it only matters that you aspire to step upon the path and do so. You can always get there from wherever you are, although, those who are just starting will have to go through most of the steps, or courses of magical development, that those already on the path have already mastered. Still, to aspire to elven magic almost always indicates an individual who has been on the path in some way or another for lifetimes, for ages, for eons. This is a deep magic, ancient and powerful and it attracts ancient souls. You feel that, don't you? You may doubt but deep within you feel it, you hope that it is true, you wish it to be and that wish is an act of magic bringing to fruition ages of preparation and calling you once again, over and over, onto the path of the elvish initiate, onto the Elven Way.

No one can prevent you from attaining power you have earned. This is not about someone external bestowing power upon you, although there are blessings one can receive and some of the greatest of these are the mentorship and guidance of the Shining Ones. All power that is given is loaned to you. It is temporarily placed in your care to be used for the accomplishment of this or that goal. But true power, the power of your unique individual s'elfhood can only be earned. Neither can others take it away, but it can be suppressed at times, often for the purpose of developing other powers, and sometimes one, quite foolishly, throws it away by neglecting it. Still, it is your magic, your power, and whether you have it, or lose it, is always your doing and a result of your own actions.

Realize this truth; it is vital. You are responsible for all that happens to you. Not because your magic created it all. Surely yours is not the only magic in the Universe, but because in the end it is you who must master the situation, master your life, master your energy and you can only do that by accepting responsibility, not blame, someone else may be to blame, but the responsibility for setting it right is yours. Surely, those who spend most of their time screwing up the world aren't about to set it in order no matter how much and often they may claim they can do so.

Fortunately, you are not alone in this. We can combine our magics. We can't give you power but we can show you the way to attain it and use it. And we can use it in concert, doing things together that we cannot at this point, or perhaps ever, accomplish alone. And we need you. Do you understand? We are family and we need every member of that family to be as powerful as they can be. That's why Faerie calls to you. We need you. We need you to unite your power with ours, to be the most powerful you can be, to contribute your unique abilities and perspective to the effort to create Elfin. It's probably not your fault the world is the way it is, but are you willing to share the responsibility to make it better?

Yet, while it is unusual, it is possible for an elven adept to be a solitary practitioner. By this we mean, not only that the elf practices hir magic alone, as many of us do starting out because we can find no brothers or sisters in our immediate vicinity, but also that the magician/witch/wizard chooses to act strictly on hir own. One is not required to work in concert with the rest of us, but it is seldom the case that elves willingly work alone, for most of us hunger for our kindred. And though one doesn't have to work with other fae, it certainly helps to do so. And in the long run, unless one intends to live in a Universe composed

The Elven Way

only of ones'elf, the elf will have to learn to be increasingly cooperative and symbiotic with all other beings. However, the more we are able to do this, which also is an indication of how advanced we are as adepts, the easier life becomes and what we desire comes to us increasingly of its own accord.

However, assuming responsibility for our lives, for our magic, requires certain things of us. The first of these is the right intent. It is vital that the elven adept adheres to what is fair for all whether sHe does hir magic with others or not. We are interconnected and it is important for every adept to realize this is so.

Elves make a basic assumption that every being is, in its primordial essence, good and pure. Its impulses are natural. It wants to succeed, its wants to be happy, which is what really is meant by and constitutes success, and it wants to live forever, to attain conscious immortality. One proceeds from this, and in the course of evolution encounters other beings, doing their own magic to obtain their goals. At this point various spells often get entangled. People begin mistakenly to think they are in eternal competition and conflict and that they can only achieve their success at the expense of others. In time, however, we realize that this state of affairs only winds up getting us trapped in magics that increasingly bind us; and the only way out of the situation is through cooperative action. We are connected to all things in the Universe and the only way for any of us to truly succeed is for all of us to do so. Therefore we add to our original impulses the addendum, *and it harm none*. We can only become unique individual's, our own true s'elves, by allowing others to do the same.

This brings us to the need for renunciation. That is to say giving up working only for one's own s'elf or group and doing what is right for all concerned. Thus we renounce our tendency to vie with others. This is achieved by reigning in our passions and desires so that while we know what they are, they don't control and drive us like a runaway horse. These desires are energies in and of themselves. Some of them are demons, really, wishing us ill and driving us to do things that are not only bad for others but which rebound on our own s'elves with terrible consequences. Some of them are relatively harmless, but can be destructive to us if allowed to gain power over us. And all of them need our guidance, we in this case being the Shining One in relationship to them, to function in a balanced way. Many high sages master these by becoming utterly without desire. But we elves are for the most part magician enchanters, and we do not eschew desire, we accept it but seek ever to master it. Thus while we may not have entirely achieved "desirelessness" that is said to be a source of magic and contentment, that is to say being satisfied and seeing as perfect all that happens in the world, we do come to view our desires in the same way we view our thoughts as we mediate, as passing phenomena to which we do not cling, and which have no power over us. Although we may, if we so choose, focus and concentrate on a thought and/or desire if doing so will help achieve a particular magical effect.

Which leads us to mastery or power. We need power to master desire. We must become masters of this power, but without it, without this will power, we become utterly the pawn of the forces of the world and our own weak character. It is a curious conundrum that we obtain power by mastering our desires and impulses yet we need power to do this very thing. But no one comes into this life utterly without power. The Life-force within us, our own spirit, which is our will to be, are great powers that have developed over the eons to bring us where we manifest currently. We have used this analogy previously, but obtaining power is like lifting weights. How do you get strong enough to lift weights? By lifting weights and increasing your strength over time. How do we obtain magical power? By using our magical power to transform ours'elves and our lives and thus gaining greater power to do even more.

This is High Elven Magic. Beginners and even some intermediate magicians think in terms of spells, chants, ceremonies and rituals, and so forth. And these symbols with which we communicate with the spirit world and thus our unconscious are significant. But the higher powers always come from the Mastery of our s'elves, for the way to power is within us. We are connected to all things in the Universe and thus have access to it from within. If we can master ours'elves all knowledge and power open up to us.

This brings us to the importance of energy and effort. We have to put in the effort to obtain the power we desire. If we wish magical power, we need to do magic. If you wish to learn to play the piano, to master the piano, you have to practice playing the piano, regularly, consistently, and with ever an eye to improving one's technique and ability. It is true that some people will be better at this than others, almost from what seems to be the start. Just as some are naturals at playing the piano and others struggle with it. But that just means they have already put in lifetimes of effort, which now manifests as *precocious talent*. The same is true for mastery of any and every kind. We were all beginners at some point, in this or a previous lifetime and we only get better by continuing to practice, which is to say do, although we elves like the word play. Some are masters of playing the piano; we become masters of playing the magic. And it is by playing the magic that we become masters.

Magical Shift of Consciousness

In Carlos Castaneda's Sorcery books, Don Juan says sorcery is a feat of shifting one's assemblage point, that is coming to a new way to viewing and experiencing the world, a shift of perception, and a restructuring of the synaptic connections in our brains, and a reorientation of the reticular formation what filters all we perceive and which is the reason words associated with our interests pop out at us when you see them in books or elsewhere. This is perhaps the greatest gift of the Shining Ones. They illuminate our consciousness, enlightening us so that we literally see the world in a new way. This is not merely a change of opinion, but a new way of experiencing the world. For the elf it means beginning to see the Faerie realms that are invisible to most folks but are ever around for those who are aware, who have the Sight. The Shining Ones gift us the sight.

Yet, though they may gift us the sight, it is we who have to develop it, otherwise it quickly fades. Perhaps, it would be more accurate to say they gift us with a glimpse of Elfin; it is we who must expand that glimpse into a full view and the ability to see it whenever we choose.

In some ways, this involves the development of maturity in the magician, but in another way it is the reclaiming of what was easy and natural when we were children. When we are children we are recapitulating earlier lifetimes when magic had greater influence in our world and was easier to see. In time, and through the process of the development of the mental aspects of the 5th root race, this ability to see magic easily was lost for most folks. But this is only a temporary and necessary phase of development so we can develop our mental facilities, and as we progress we regain this capacity that came so naturally for most of us as children with the addition of reasoning ability, logic and greater maturity. Thus the great sages are often child-like but not childish.

We begin to distinguish between temporary truths and the facts of terrestrial existence from absolute truth, the truths of the Universe through eternity. We increasingly become able to understand things, and people, from the perspective of lifetimes of development. We are able to not only see how they are currently, but how they got to be there, and where they are likely to proceed, considering their current trajectory, as well as their ultimate destination. This makes us seem like prophets and sooth-sayers, which we are, but really we are only examining the truths of evolutionary development on the micro and macro scales. This is not so much or not entirely a psychic phenomena but an esoteric understanding of the facts of reality and the nature of the Universe.

The elven adept understands the illusionary nature of the world, and the underlying purity of being that lives within it and from which it springs, but at the same time seeks to create a world, an illusion so to speak, a glamor, a matrix of being that is beautiful and fulfilling for all to see and experience. Faerie is a work of art and we the artists. Just as we know a masterpiece by a great painter is composed of plain canvas and pure paint, we know Faerie is created from pure undifferentiated energy. For as canvas and paint, what are they but potentiality? It is the masterpiece we seek to bring into existence. The masterpiece of creativity that we call Faerie or Elfin.

From this new and higher perspective or Sight comes attitude. Our attitude becomes filled with illuminated energy, or is energized by illumination and from this attitude, this spirit, our actions, which is to say our magic, flows. This attitude is not primarily a mental point of view. It is not about someone saying that we should view things this or that way, but about a real inclination of the individual elf to act and respond to the world. Many people say that they are one thing or one way, or that they believe or disbelieve this or that, but then something happens and they react in a totally different way contrary to their stated beliefs. Their stated philosophy contradicted by their inner intent and inclination. As elven adept we bring these things in harmony with each other.

Attitude is deeper than belief. It arises from the inner spirit and it creates an atmosphere, an ambience around one. It is magic. It affects one environment. Have you noticed how depressed people can be so depressing? Have you noted that certain individuals just make you want to laugh, or lift your spirits without even trying, simply by being thems'elves? The attitude of the elfin adept is one of empowerment and confidence and thus the elven adept instills others with confidence as well. As the elf progresses in the magic, obtains a certain level of mastery, sHe cannot help but feel more confident as an enchanter magician witch sorcerer or whatever. This confidence inspires others. They can see, and more importantly they can feel that the magic is real for the magician is living it. It hums through hir life and affects all sHe encounters thus empowering those who are open and ready for such upliftment.

From this basic attitude that exudes confidence and which empowers others, more individualized attitudes develop as well. The elf is serene, or focused and seriously devoted to the quest. The elf is joyful and ever happy. These sub-attitudes are a function of personality, which in itself is an effect of the adept's mastery and spirit. Personality is a power. It moves and affects people. It attracts certain spirits to one. Ever hear of someone who has been described as having "no personality"? What is meant by that except that the individual is dull and tends to dissolve into the background, having no affect on hir environment, thus no magic, fading slowly into the void of robot-hood. Welcome to the Borg. Welcome to normal humanity or the way the dark sorcerer's would like normal to be. Willing and eager slaves saying, "Yes sir, Master."

The elfin adept's personality is more powerful than circumstances. It is what carries the elf through difficult times; it is what inspires others in those times. In mastering yours'elf, your desires, your weakness, in facing and developing yours'elf to overcome your limitations, seek ever to develop your personality, establish a successful and confident attitude, for these are the outward presentation of your spirit. It is the light of the fire that burns within you, that bit of flame born from the Sacred Silver Flame of Elfin.

From attitude springs intent and motivation, or is it the other way around? Intent is vital to magic, particularly elven magic. We need ask ours'elves what it is we really wish to achieve both on the small and large scale. When your intent is in harmony with the urge toward light and realization that permeates the Universe, we put ours'elves in touch with the Divine Faerie Magic and go with the flow of evolutionary development.

So, too, must we become aware of our motivations. Why do we do what we do? What is motivating you? In answering this question we come to the aspect of renunciation.

Letting Go of the Small to Attain the Great

Much of the world looks at the resources around us like a pie that has to be split up among so many people with each wanting the biggest slice of the pie, and some not getting any at all, which the dark magicians say is their own fault for being too weak to take it by force.

This point of view is not without validity or truth, although its validity comes from those who ascribe to it, so they can have a slice of the pie. And its truth is a transitory truth, a little truth that fails to see the greater truth that the Universe is ever abundant and there is more than enough energy for everyone.

This temporary truth is answered by the elves with the more eternal truths of sustainability and renewability. We also respond to this temporary fact of terrestrial existence with the magical act of sharing. As we elves say, "When we share, we all have more."

Most spiritual and religious philosophies deal with these things by means of out and out renunciation. One surrenders one's will to God, relinquishes personal desires and possessions for the greater good. Alas, as we've noted that usually means giving up what you have so someone at the top can have more, and relinquishing your will power so someone supposedly closer to God can tell you what to do. However, in pointing this out, we do not wish to denigrate those saintly individuals who do this with the best of intentions and sometimes with good, which is to say truly beneficial, results.

But the elves are not inclined for the most part to give up our innocent and natural desires, but we do see the world in a larger context. We come to know as adepts that to achieve what we truly desire, which for the most part is a more loving and magical world, everyone else has to find hir own happiness as well. We know that in a more loving world, we are more likely to get what we want as individuals and as a group.

We achieve this through renunciation of the small for the greater. We forgo what is near for what is afar. For instance, many elves, as well as other folk, raised in the world where bullies seem to be everywhere, even on the internet, and one-up-man-ship an accepted, even encouraged, part of life, often feel a lack of s'elf esteem at first. These elves struggle, along with the masses, for recognition. They want to join the few who have been accorded by society to be worthy of acknowledgement and praise. Thus these often present thems'elves to be more than they are, flaunting their ego for all to see. But elven adepts have found for the most part that we don't attain this by asking for it but by renouncing it. It is another curious fact that this culture of dominance tends to give freely to those who already have more than they can ever use and to withhold its benefits from those who most need it and ask for it.

Thus to gain recognition, elven adepts pursue their work without pursuing praise and if offered praise are ever modest about accepting it, which has the magical effect of making the individuals give them even more praise. Yes, it is an elf trick. But a clever one, no? Be ever modest and the recognition for which you have so hungered will come to you.

We are often told by spiritual and religious types that we should give up our ego, our sense of s'elf, but for elves this means relinquishing our divisive ego, that is the tendency to see ours'elves as separate from others, and the temptation to assert our ego to demonstrate our worth by proving we are better than others. This is a trap placed by the dark magicians to ensnare us to either push ours'elves forward at the expense of others or yield our s'elfhood in subservience to them. Neither is appropriate for the elf.

For us, ego is about what psychologists refer to as ego-strength, a positive sense of our s'elf, our value as human or non-human beings, our confidence in ours'elves, without placing our unique s'elfhood in competition with others. How can we really? We are unique. We cannot really be compared. We are neither above them, nor below them. We are always and ever our own true s'elves. We are special and in a category all our own. It's not so much that they broke the mold after making us, but that the mold that forms us is transformative in nature. It shape-shifts continually; it mutates constantly, producing a series of ever-unique individuals.

So what do we renounce? First of all we renounce the temptation to vie with others. It is not that we don't ever compete, but it is always fair competition, what used to be called sportsman-like competition. We know that success comes when we all succeed, thus we share our success. We are more about playing the game, and being good at playing the game, than winning. Men and others say that winning is everything, we elves believe that playing that game well is everything and that's how we win. Beyond any little games we might engage in, we are always playing the big game, the Game of Life, the Master Game. Winning friendship is always our goal.

It is not that we are never called to make sacrifices. Life offers that opportunity to all of us. But true sacrifice is always voluntary and always of the s'elf or what we have. You can't take something from someone else and have it be true sacrifice. That is an illusion, a spell of entrapment created by the dark sorcerers for those who feel too selfish to give freely.

However, know that sacrifice nearly always is prompted by love. It is like parents who save up to get that piano or other instrument for which their beloved child hungers, or save for tuition for a better school, or college to uplift their child. Just as a person in love sacrifices for their beloved, so do we elves sacrifice for our beloved, which are the spirits and souls struggling for enlightenment in darkness of the material world, where the shadows are born. We give to gain something better, something more important. We renounce what is near for what is far, what is small for what is great, and we do so out of love. Love and friendship are the motivations that prompt the elf to nearly every action. What else is there worth doing? Without it life becomes empty and meaningless.

But this is the reality. We give to gain something greater. We give for love and gain love in giving. Not buying love, as some try to do, but gain it by giving it. Our act of love is the love we are gifted. And as our dear elf brother Jesus demonstrated, in giving we gain so much more.

This is the secret magic of renunciation. Just as we gain praise in forgoing it, we gain love by giving out of love. We gain confidence by not needing to vie with others, or create factions, and then all we will comes to us by magic when we realize we already have it in abundance. It's just waiting out there as unrealized potentiality in the Universe.

It is not that we should be wasteful or unwise in our giving. We should always endeavor to make our gifting count. But we should not refrain from giving when we have so much, neither should we fear to share when we have little, for in both instances renunciation and sacrifice will bring us more.

We know, we can hear their voices in the distance, saying, "New Age Poppycock." And to them this is true. These are often the same ones who spend time in their church, mosque or synagogue acting fervent for social recognition and then going forth again to act with greed, hate, violence and other aspects of behavior directly in contrast to the precepts of their religion. They are caught in and at the same time reinforcing a dark spell of cynicism that traps them into a self-fulfilling prophecy of the world where one must always watch one's back and no one can really be trusted. Their magic creates their world just as ours creates our realms.

We also live out s'elf fulfilling prophecies. Only our prophecies are of evolutionary development, of the transformation of the soulful spirit toward more loving behavior, of the success of magic bringing us blessings and luck.

It is true, particularly here in the material world where different magics struggle to weave thems'elves into a consistent tapestry that we may be affected by, or suffer due to, their magics. We, too, are prone to the limitations of this world, the sufferings that others endure, the pain that others inflict. But, that being said, we elves are luckier than most. Our magic, while not all powerful, shapes our world the best it can and we get the best from it. Our renunciations made with love help balance our karma and we grow in time to be ever more powerful. Which brings us again to the aspect of power.

Using Power

We elves, like nearly every other spirit in the Universe, seek power, which is to say the power to succeed, the power to obtain happiness. Who wishes to be utterly dependent upon others? And yet we are at certain times. Or at least seem to be.

Take babies for instance. As babies we seem to be utterly in the power of others to care for us or neglect us according to their own situation or disposition. Of course, while we may seem powerless in that situation, the elves know that this is not entirely the case. We are first and foremost in the grip of our own karma. That is to say what happens to us as babies in part reflects the recoil of our own magic in previous lifetimes.

And while we may seem powerless as babies, elf and other babies often give off pheromones (faerie moans) that cast a spell on our caretakers inclining them to adore us, nurture us and even die for us if need be to protect us. How's that for magical power?

Like most people we seek to succeed in the world, but it is

quite likely that most elves regard that success quite differently than the majority of folks. What seems to many to be the ever elusive values of happiness and true love, also stand at the center of our vision, but for us they are primary values and material success and social recognition rate far beneath them and only really have value in as much as they help us achieve love and happiness.

We've have heard again and again that many a wealthy person, many a famous person, many a successful business person, many of those who have obtained fame are then so miserable that they commit suicide, because after having achieved everything in the world they believed would give them happiness, they had still not obtained it. They realize, usually too late for this particular life, that what they were told and what they believed would bring happiness simply didn't do so. And despite what some people of maudlin or severe disposition claim, happiness is a primary goal of all beings in the Universe (see our book *Through the Mists of Faerie* or our *Book of Elven Magick, 1 & 2* for more on this). The other primary goal is, of course, Immortality.

People will gladly and willingly sacrifice nearly anything for those they truly love, those who bring them joy and happiness. As elves we also sacrifice for our loved ones, but on the other side of that equation we seek to become as adorable as possible. Exactly that, adorable, just like that cute baby you'd die for. We do all we can to be enchanting, to be givers of joy, not only because this is a joyous thing to do, but also because we know it is a great power and we further know that all true power stems from the development of our spirit, of our unique s'elfhood, of our personality. Remember, we elves are first, foremost and primarily enchanters.

There are those who eschew power in the world. They say, "Money is the root of all Evil", and "Power corrupts and Absolute Power corrupts absolutely" and so on. And certainly there are dangers involved in the acquisition, possession and use of money and power. But we elves also know that we are destined to be powerful. We are destined, at the same time, to have absolute abundance at our disposal. And most of all we are destined to use these to bring beauty and fairness into the world, to make it a more magical place for everyone. What is Faerie about if not to bring enchantment to the world, making it a better world, a more beautiful world, where everyone gets hir just desserts, good or bad.

What is power really? It is the skill to take the primal Divine Magic that manifests in the world as energy, accumulate it and direct it toward the realization of our goals. How do we acquire power? We do it primarily by perfecting our s'elves for the energy is all around us, everywhere, at all times, it is we who must develop our vehicles, our body, mind, feelings and soulful spirit to be fit receivers and transformers of this energy. This means not only being of a powerful nature, a powerful personality but furthermore having the enlightened disposition and maturity to use it wisely.

In the true nature of the Universe, all things are possible and exist as potentiality. That is to say they live in the place where they both are and are not at the same time. That is the place we transverse from life to death and back again. Among all those possibilities, and remember everything imaginable is possible, we chose by our actions, which are our magics, to bring some of those possibilities into manifestation. We elves chose to manifest Faerie because of its wonder and beauty and its nature that nurtures all.

Thus once again we say that while Faerie exists in potentiality apart from us, it is brought into manifestation through us. We give it life. We wish it into existence. We are elves and this is our magic. This is our power.

We seek ever to create a more beautiful, loving, kind and creative world. In doing so, we do not demand that others participate or insist that they live in the same way. In fact, this is ultimately impossible since every spirit creates its own world, although due to our soulful connections most of these worlds, these dimensions overlap, intermingle and in places merge. Love binds us, and our worlds, together.

Thus we are connected, and yes karmically, to everyone and everything in our Universe. You could say they are all a part of us, certainly in a sense they are all related to us, they are all part of a vast extended family, whether they realize it or not, or like it or not. This may seem like a bad thing to some since there are many denizen of this world and Universe who seem less than disposed toward us in a kindly way, but this is also a good thing because it means we have access to everything in the Universe, all knowledge and all power, because of our relationship to it. Without that relationship, we couldn't possibly obtain it. And though, at this point, it may seem that much of the Universe is only tenuously connected to us, and this is also to our benefit, and some of it seeks to prey on us, we are meant to master all these things, and in doing so gain greater power, and in gaining greater power master more. We are becoming Divine Magical beings and with that comes tremendous power. Although, alas, the opposite is not necessarily true. One can gain great power without developing one's Divine Nature, although the consequences of this in the long run, as we've previously stated prove devastating to the individual, for such individuals undermine themselves in the long run, diminishing the Divine Spark within them, and undoing themselves. Thus power with proper intention is increasingly important as one ascends into the ranks of the Shining Ones. It is the avenue to success, the key to knowledge and power, and our protection.

Mastering our vehicles is, as noted, important, but we must also master our technique, or skill in the magical mystical spiritual arts. There is a reason that the world Wizard, and there are many elfin wizards, means both a practitioner of a particular form of magic and someone who is a genius or a wizard at doing things. The word combines magic and expertise and this is no accident. We learn to use power wisely, but we also learn to use it well, efficiently, effectively and with elegance and grace. We ever seek to refine what we do and the way we do it.

Creativity is most important. The unique and the original are greatly valued. It doesn't have to be refined if it has genuine style. The elves value style above technique. However, when style is refined it is greater yet, while technique and refinement without style or substance fails to move us. Thus what the Shining Ones wish most for us is that each of us develops and contributes our unique style to the Great Magic, but then having done that they expect and encourage us to refine it, to make it in this way more powerful. In that sense, we all eventually become wizards at being enchanters.

The fact that we, as yet, are not all powerful, or nearly so, able to get whatever we wish at any time instantly is only to say we are, first, not all we will eventually be, and second, the world would become pretty dull rather quickly without any challenges before us. Why do you think we descended into this gravity well in the first place? This is the cosmic drama and we are here to live it and master it from the inside out. In some ways we are like the boss's children who are working at every job in the factory or business until we know the place from bottom to top and will be prepared to run it when our time comes. In another sense, we are like divine magicians who have cast a spell of forgetfulness over ours'elves so we can enjoy the quest to discover our true s'elves, overcome every challenge and master the material and other dimensions. We live in a matrix of our own creation, a movie we have chosen to go to, but instead of merely watching it, it is a virtual reality movie that we participate in, a holodeck we are exploring after intentionally giving ours'elves amnesia, or as some call it, dying and being born again, or manifesting on the wheel of reincarnation.

Let us remind you at this point that as you grow more powerful you will be able to enter the Faerie dimensions that are more dreamlike in essence, being as they are, closer to the Source of All Magic, which is to say pure potentiality. When we say dream-like we mean that it feels real, just like this world you are currently in, just as a dream feels real when you are in it and it is just as real and just as illusionary as these worlds, but it will be a world in which you have more and more power. You will be able to fly, or walk through walls or have amazing things happen, just as in dreams. As we say, it will be just as real, actually more real, than the mundane world that is so distant from the Source and so cluttered with magical knots and entanglements that it is sluggish and slow.

As you gain power, you will in the course of time, slip from one world to another, not only stepping from parallel world to parallel world due to your decisions, but also from the mundane realm where your magic is bound or tied up to the more permeable realms where your magic will be freer and you will be able to accomplish more, and yes, be able to thus affect the mundane realm from that one. You may at some point abandon the mundane world altogether when you get powerful enough, but that is up to you and usually a decision made based on love. The Shining Ones who abide here do so because they love us, and we in turn will stay or go according to the love we have for our kindred who are still bound here.

You might think of being in those worlds as equivalent to being in a lucid dream and at the same time you might practice the technique of viewing the mundane world as a lucid dream as one of the magical techniques you can use to develop the power to go there. Another key, among many really, is the imaginal power, the ability to visualize and use your imagination, stepping into the imaginal realm with the ease that most children do. This is in part why many of the best books on magic, particularly but not exclusively elven faerie magic, are works of fiction, especially those for young adult readers. If a fantasy story evokes your imagination, you are dealing with real magic.

Day dreaming, however, is a double edge sword. In some ways it is harmless, but that's its problem, it is often a means to balance our sense of inadequacies, our hunger for true love, to be heroic, to have wealth, etc. that we feel we are lacking on the mundane plane. However, unless we use this facility with power, with magic, it merely becomes a waste of our time and energy, so while it is not bad essentially, it drains our energy. Still, despair not. If you have an active fantasy life, as some of us here do, it is a good sign of a productive imagination and when developed will turn into real power. For the imaginal realm is one of the keys to entering the shamanic realms of vision and power that lead us to Faerie.

So while guiding and developing this power you don't wish to prevent it from happening. It's rather like thoughts in meditation. You don't prevent them, you don't struggle with them, you just watch them go by while continuing to focus. Don't think of controlling your fantasies but channeling them toward your magical practice. Of course, anything you can do to work on lucid dreaming, out of the body experience, or really any of the other magical powers you have or are developing is the right thing to do.

Your powers, after all, are not going to be exactly like everyone else's. While you can learn nearly all magics, you will find that certain ones come naturally to you and these are often based upon your uniqueness, your foibles, your peculiarities, or even what most people see to be your disabilities. Just as the blind often have a keener sense of hearing and/or smell, so do each of us develop compensatory magical skills that balance out what seems to be some inadequacy in the mundane realms.

Still, it behooves us to develop ours'elves in everyway we can. To strengthen what is weak in us, replace ignorance with knowledge and in all ways make ours'elves better and to refine and improve the skills we already have. It is a curious aspect of the Universe that we are perfect as we are and yet, if we are wise, ever improving ours'elves. Thus we elves in looking into the world see the perfection of each being, and at the same time, sense how each might become even more. We might compare this to cutting and polishing diamonds. Many of us are diamonds in the raw, uncut, yet perfect in our way. Some of us are cut diamonds needing but a bit of polish. Yet, all of us are diamonds/soulful spirits.

Faerie is sometimes called the Perilous Realm; and for those who aren't ready, who don't have the sufficient power or maturity, it can certainly be so. That is why in part it is so important to develop control over one's own being, one's mind, feelings, and intentions. In a world in which one's thoughts, or desires, or wishes come near to instantly manifesting, it is dangerous to have miscellaneous ideas cropping up. One's fears will manifest. One's worries will be called into being. As dangerous as the material world may be at times, it is nothing compared to going unprepared into the Faerie realms and it thus serves as a protection and a barrier to our own negative or uncontrolled thinking by delaying their actualization.

In the material world if you have a nightmare, you wake up. To wake up from a nightmare of Faerie, which in part is what a dream really is, a trip to Faerie, you are cast into the material world. To wake up from a nightmare, a real nightmare, in the material realm, one dies, returns to the realm of pure potentiality, and is reborn. So again we say to you, do all you can to master your thoughts, desires and other aspects of your being or your stay in Faerie will be short, and you will be glad to be out of there.

However, once you have the power and maturity and development to stay, it can become the most marvelous of realms. But that, of course, is up to you. It is your magic that is a major part of creating it.

In the meantime, you may wish to appreciate the relative safety of the mundane world that is slow and limited and buffered a great deal for our protection. We know you are probably eager to get out of the crib, but it's there for a reason, and yes, one can still die in the crib, in fact, we all do eventually, over and over again. It is a good place to learn our magic.

Certainty

Some folks think that magic is based on faith or belief, and while both of these can be tremendously powerful, they are not the source of power. Faith is a great thing, as is belief, although many folks have beliefs and faith in things that are but illusions. But then, as we've said, we are, in part, in the business of creating glamor and illusions. So faith can be quite potent in that respect.

However, more powerful in our experience is certainty and certainty usually comes from experience. One does magic, sees what the results are and comes to understand one's powers and limitations at a particular point and time. Certainty gives one power.

On the other hand, faith and belief that one can be more, do greater, is important as well. Certainty is derived from scientific experimentation and research, that is to say you do magic and note the results. Faith and belief are aspects of the art of magic. We blend these things together, the scientific and the artistic, to create a balanced magic. We do not ignore experience, or reality, but we also do not ignore the imaginal, the possible, and the as yet unknown. In fact, it is the driving passion of science to ever explore the unknown to achieve ever-greater knowledge. This is true of the esoteric paths as well as the exoteric ones.

Courage

Developing power requires a certain amount of courage. Certainly, stepping into the Perilous Faerie realms does and one needs power to do that and stay there for any length of time.

The majority of folk often scorn the powers that we use, the powers of courtesy, kindness, and other aspects of enchantment. Esoteric lore itself is often ridiculed, magic laughed at, and elves for the most part are not given any regard at all. It takes great courage to persevere on a path that most consider only worthy of their scorn and ridicule.

It is not that we don't value the things that they value. We understand the importance of money, social position, and so on, but we also value knowledge, love, loyalty and enlightenment and the development of the unique aspects of the individual even more. And we also value things that they, for the most part, seem to no longer concern themselves with at all, such as honor, which they consider old fashioned and irrelevant. It takes courage to pursue this path when the mass of humanity considers it worthless and some even consider it evil.

And part of this courage is not only braving the scorn of others, facing the danger to sanity that one may expose ones'elf to in entering faerie, but also the courage to persevere when progress takes such a very long time. This is a path of lifetimes upon lifetimes. It requires a particular courage called patience and persistence. One must endure. Before we fly as magicians, we must run; before we run, we walk; before we walk, we crawl.

We must also develop the courage, some might say wisdom, to put aside our personal ego, our sense of self-importance, our need for recognition, so we can accept the positive direction of those who seek to nurture and guide us. The Elven Adept becomes so eager to learn that sHe thanks everyone who corrects hir every error. For in doing so sHe becomes ever better and more powerful. We are eager to correct our errors, eager to improve our game, our ability, our knowledge, our magic in every way possible, not to raise ours'elves above others but to more effectively merge with them. And remember, all things, all knowledge, all experience, all power comes from loving and harmonious, thus soulful, union.

In a certain sense, Elfin magic is ever and always interconnected magic. It is at its heart the magic of friendship, family, love and association. We increasingly become a part of the web-work of Faerie, the esoteric ley-lines of magical potency, weaving our lives together to create through our union something truly wondrous and magical.

Energy

Magic, like all things, and to the elves all things are magic, takes an investment of time and energy. One must put in the effort. Just as one must invest in a business to get it started and make it thrive, one must invest in Faerie magic, and in one's spiritual life. Only, an investment in the world is, for the most part a transitory phenomena, while an investment in one's spirit is an investment in eternity.

Magic is often defined as getting what one desires using will power. There is surely truth to this, but we could also say that magic is action. Magic stems from our choices. The magician chooses and acts, thus putting energy toward hir choice. The Zen magician, represented by the Fool in the tarot, does the opposite. SHe considers the world perfect and does nothing to alter it, allowing it to do and become whatever it will. Hirs is a magic of acceptance, non-action, and non-interference.

We elves tend to balance these things. We act, do magic, influencing the Universe toward granting our will, our desires, and sometimes we allow, we let things happen. We are ever aware that ours is not the only magic and in fact, all things considered, our magic is very small, compared to the whole. Yet, still our magic requires energy, to do or refrain from doing, requires choice and effort, even if it is the effort of restraint.

As we said earlier, we elves are not entirely fond of the connotations often associated with the word work in normal society. It often implies something that one doesn't wish to do, doesn't enjoy doing, or does only for financial gain, or because one is forced to do it. In our society, work and play are blended ideas. We make all we do enjoyable and endeavor to enjoy all we do. That does not mean we are sloppy at what we do, rather it means that in the doing it, we always do our every best. The dedication and energy that is typically associated with playing sports in normal society is closer to our idea of work.

Thus as we becoming increasingly powerful, the energy we put into our magic becomes ever more efficient, that is we get the most from the least needed, and we become ever more proficient at doing it; thus while it still takes effort, energy, it stems from our natural movements, is part of our very life. Elven magic follows the path of least resistance. It flows like a river. It rises toward the morning sun like the mist, becoming ever more invisible, insubstantial and "transmutating" from the material to the energetic spiritual dimensions. Our effort becomes effortless. We merge the action of the magician with the non-action of the Zen master; all stems naturally from our own natures. We are true to ours'elves in all things and all we do originates from the increasing purity of our being.

We do not interfere with the Universe or Nature, we join it, cooperate with it, find or create our own perfect place within it, and all things become as they should be, which they potentially already are, we just have to realize it, that is make it real in our own lives.

Our energy, however, is nearly always positive energy, by which we mean it is ever directed toward the fulfillment of our own creative goals. We don't waste our time interfering with others, unless the Universe, the Shining Ones give us a duty to do so. But our intention is always toward creation and such, shall we say weed pulling, is only done when necessary. There are those, it is true, who will be joining the Lords of Karma, and these have a more natural tendency in this direction, toward adjusting the balance. We each find our perfect place by becoming perfectly ours'elves.

Our greatest investment of energy, which is also our greatest magical power, our most profound magical perspective, and the thing for which we renounce all other things, is Love. Love, friendship, family are keys to elven magic and the Elven Way can be explained very simply by evoking those powers and combining them with the ancillary aspects of loyalty, nurturing and honor and a good bit of style. Faerie is about family. Faerie is about love.

Of course, there are some that will tell you otherwise. They view elves as the petty squabblers (actually a type of goblin) that the Unseelie are portrayed as being, endlessly struggling over territory and domain. Or as the elementals that are vast and incredible powers that are impersonal in their actions destroying good with bad as they proceed on their course, as a volcano or hurricane seems to do. Or as the petty gods they so often say they worship who torture you if you fail to believe in or acknowledge them, or if they think you insult them in some way. And all these things have truth to them, but it is a small truth, as petty as the instincts from which they originate. True High Elven Magic is about Love, simply and completely that. It is our great power and we put all our energy into creating it and all that we create we attempt to do with love. When you understand that and pursue it, put your own energy ceaseless toward it, you have stepped upon the Elven Way and are in the process of becoming an adept elven enchanter.

At the same time, if you are anything like us you might pause at this moment, wonder if there is a slight hint of olde time religion or New Age pablum in this and begin to taste a slight gorge at the back of your throat and be fighting a tendency to want to regurgitate. We understand. We really do.

But the Elven Way is not a religion. There is no one to worship, although we suggest you try worshipping everyone. There are no religious rites to follow, save those rites of magic you create for yours'elf. There are no spiritual holidays to celebrate, although we elves like to celebrate everyday and will share any holiday, religious or secular, that involves joyous union and consider it an elven holiday. There are no prohibitions, though we do suggest that helping others is wiser than interfering with them. No food taboos, but becoming vegetarian does seem to be most in keeping with our evolutionary goals. No priests or priestesses, although if someone wishes to maintain and run a sanctuary for the rest of us that seems a pretty nice thing to do. No dress code but this, wear what pleases you and encourage others to do the same. No uniform ceremonial vestments save what looks cool and magical, wizardly, sorcerous and elven. No doctrine save be the best friend you can be to everyone open to true friendship. And there is no particular way to be, beyond being our own true s'elf. And again, if you can do all this with a bit of love, style and panache, that is elven enough for us.

Many people, and many novels about magic, warn us that magic costs. By this they mean that for whatever powers we have or use we will suffer or be punished for using them. It is true that magic cost, that is to say it requires energy from us, an investment of time and effort, but if done well it profits us even more. That is the whole idea, to invest in Faery, in our soulful spirits, and become even greater thereby. Don't believe those who try to scare you from doing your magic. Elfin magic is only truly dangerous if your intentions are wrong. Others, it is true may endanger you, but they can only harm your body they can't really do anything to your soul or spirit, only you can do that. The dark spells that warn you against magic are just that, dark spells meant to entangle one in the beliefs and dogmas of others, which at the same time are used by the Shining Ones to filter out those who do not have the sufficient daring to enter Faery. Do you dare enter the realms of the Shining Ones?

The Elven Way

WHAT DOES FAERIE ASK OF US?
WHAT DOES IT REQUIRE?
BUT FOR US TO BE OUR OWN TRUE S'ELVES
FULFILL OUR HEARTS' DESIRE
TO MASTER OURS'ELVES PERFECTLY
OR BEST THAT WE ARE ABLE
TO BE ADEPT IN WHAT WE DO
INVOKE THE ANCIENT FABLE
WE ARE THE FAERIE TALES
COME TRUE
WE ARE THE WISH THAT'S GRANTED
WE ARE THE BLOSSOM MAGICAL
FROM ELFIN SEEDS WE'VE PLANTED
WE ARE THE LIVING FAERIE
WE ARE THE VISION REAL
WE ARE WHAT THEY HAVE FANTASIZED
OF WHAT THEY WISH TO FEEL
WE ARE THE MAGIC FORMULA
WE ARE THE SPELL THAT'S CAST
WE ARE ENCHANTMENT MANIFEST
THAT SHALL FOREVER LAST

> "Why do the Shining Ones care? Is it that we are so important? Well, we are important to them as a child is dear to its parents, as a lover to its beloved, as a family is to each other. They care because we are theirs and they ours. It is as simple and wondrous as that."
> —The Silver Elves

CHAPTER 14:
ASCENDING INTO THE REALMS OF THE SHINING ONES

We seek to discover our true nature, our divinity, our magic, the uniqueness and specialness of our own true being. We seek to become immortal, not only as spirits, but as conscious entities, that is to live forever in the same, more or less, body, or retain our consciousness lifetime after lifetime. We seek happiness, which is success, which is ecstasy. These goals are hardwired into our beings, and they are not separate, but one; we pursue each of them to obtain them all. To do this we need power, and the greatest power is the power of our true s'elf in its perfected and unique, perhaps weird, but wondrous manifestation. Thus we must increasingly do all we can to improve ours'elves in every way.

We are not alone, however; threads of love, karma and experience connect us to all that is. We come from the same source, which is the Divine Magic of Possibility in its undifferentiated state of pure energy, and we use that to create the worlds we envision. In the process of that we have become temporarily trapped in a dimension slowed by conflicting magic that has all become entangled as every spirit sought to fulfill its own vision at the same time. As we untangle these knots of magic, the energy begins to flow again, but we can only do that by cooperating with other, particularly and especially those beings who are seeking to empower each of us to fulfill ours'elves perfectly. These ancient kindred of ours we call the Shining Ones.

We are not forced to cooperate with these beings, or any

others, it is just that it is wise and more effective and efficient to do so, not simply because they are far more experienced and powerful than we, but because we come to understand that the only way this whole thing turns out well is if we each help each other to obtain what we desire.

And yet, the world we are entangled within is like a Chinese finger trap. The more one struggles and pulls the tighter it gets. To solve this puzzle one needs to relax and approach this problem with a confident and easy approach, pushing instead of pulling, giving more than taking, doing rather than waiting for it to happen. So, too, must we help others in order to help ours'elves and help ours'elves as a means to helping others. Like most things in Elfin, this is a paradox, but then Faerie is a mysterious place and we are its mysterious inhabitants. All we desire is found and achieved within ours'elves and through each other. This is what the Shining Ones understand, which is why, even though they are far advanced and evolved compared to these wee elves, they are compassionate enough to do all in their power to aid us without weakening us by doing so.

The Shining Ones are star enchanters. Yet, saying that it may sound as though they live out among the stars, which they do, but they also live in more subtle, though connected, dimensions than our own. Their world is more real and more dreamlike than ours. What they *will* comes easily to them and the typical movie or book that shows a wizard snapping his fingers to light a candle or casting a spell to create dinner, is an actuality of their world/dimension.

It is convenient for us to anthropomorphize these beings, but in truth these beings are beings of light and can materialize in any form they desire. Though most of us are far from achieving these things, they are our destiny and our future. We are gradually entering the realms of Elfin, where magic rules and love reigns and we can only find our perfect place of magical power and fulfillment by being who are truly are.

In the meantime, the neighbors are screaming at each other, the bills are coming due, and our bodies are slowly disintegrating and it is a bit hard to focus on the more magical and divine realm due to the clatter and pressure of the material world. Things are progressing so slowly that it is in fact hard at times to believe that we are evolving at all. Despite all the magical things that have happened in our lives we are still prone to doubt at times and among the many things we seek to develop in ours'elves is the faith of scientific certainty or perhaps scientific uncertainty or open-mindedness. Perseverance alone keeps us going at such times, that and our beloved kindred who, when we fade and wander away call out to us summoning us again and again unto the path, back to the Elven Way.

The world we live in is an illusion, not because it isn't real, for we experience as real, but because it is a transitory phenomena, a mere play or drama that we are enacting. Yet, it is composed of the real. The energy, the consciousness that creates this play is real, which is to say eternal and it can neither be created nor destroyed only transformed into a near infinite variety of possibilities. Yet, few of us wish to live forever in the undifferentiated homogeneity of the pure energetic consciousness. We create these worlds for a reason. We create these plays for our own joy and entertainment. We, most of us here in this dimension, are just not very powerful as yet and thus unable to manifest the world entirely to our vision or design. In time, we will not only become more powerful and therefore able to manifest what we desire, but in doing so we will migrate to those dimensions where that greater power exists, where wishes come true and dreams are realized. We call these dimensions Faerie. Or you could say that we are, in fact, already incredibly powerful but our magic is all knotted up with other beings who are also amazingly powerful. Thus our powers seem limited, but really they are only limited due to the conflicting interests of other great powers.

It would be unwise, and only serve to get us further entangled to forget that the worlds we are creating are just that, our creations, our art. It is important ever to remember what is real and true, which is the underlying pure energetic potentiality as well as the essential unity of all things. This is in part what is meant by the expression of living in the world without being of the world.

But it also helps to remember that since the world is based on pure potentiality that all we wish can come true. Although, while we often think that we are changing the world, we are in a sense traveling through the dimensions of manifest potentiality, for all things are possible, but not all are possible in the same place. Our choices, as we've said, are doorways from one parallel world to another. In changing ours'elves, we shift the world we are living within. The more we become our true s'elves the closer we become to our chosen place or path in the Universe, and thus the more intimately we connect to the pure potentiality from which all Magic/possibility stems.

Being connected to all other things and beings in our world, some more closely than others, we are also entangled in their magics. The key to untangling the magic is cooperation and detachment. By helping others achieve their true needs and desires, we combine our magics with theirs. By becoming detached from our own desires, by doing our magic from a place of ease and un-attachment, we become more flexible and adaptable. In a sense it is as though we have thus oiled ours'elves and the tangled threads of magic no longer bind us and cease to create inhibiting knots and we slip through the world easily. These knots are the effects of karma we have created from our magic/actions.

We are not saying that one should thus forgo all one's desires nor give up doing magic to achieve what one wishes, but in including the needs of others in our magic and in being flexible and adaptable in the fulfillment of our magic we get more of what we need and are better able to use all that occurs to our advantage. This adaptability is a highlight of the character of the Shining Ones who use all events to further their particular vision and include all in it; and we are wise to follow their example.

Of course, there is a limit to what we can know and say of the Shining Ones both because they are in so many instances so far beyond us that we can do little more than project from what we do know into the unknown. But also because they are increasingly unique as beings and thus cannot really fall into any categories we might project upon them. It is like trying to explain to a virgin what having sex is like. It is not only difficult because they haven't experienced it and have no real basis to attach the description of our experience, but also because the experience differs for each individual. We could say general things that are more or less true for most or we could speak of specific things that apply to our own experience, which may or may not apply to anyone else's experience, and in either case the virgin can only imagine what it is like and may encounter a totally different experience when sHe passes over the threshold from imagination into reality.

The Shining Ones are far more psychic than we, although in saying that we do not mean the sort of strained and dramatic energy that is often viewed as psychic in the movies and on television. Rather their mind-to-mind communication tends to be an increasingly powerful development of rapport on the one hand and projection on the other. Just as couples who have been together for a long time or who have a natural simpatico often finish each others sentences, and say what the other person was just thinking and so forth, so do the Shining Ones have a natural and even more powerful rapport with each other. The 6th sub-race of the 5th root race that is currently emerging upon this planet, you may call it Earth, we sometimes call it Elfin, will increasingly evolve and demonstrate this ability. And the 6th root race for which this sub-race is a precursor will have this talent in a fully developed fashion. These will be the first elves truly evidencing the powers that fantasy novels generally portray us as possessing.

Also, the Shining Ones have the ability to project thoughts from mind-to-mind that we are just beginning to develop. For them this is an easy power, and they are able to not only communicate to each other in this fashion but to impress less open minds with thoughts and ideas that may prove useful to them. However, they can do this only in the form of suggestion or inspiration since to do otherwise would override the individual's right to think for hir self. To encourage a spirit toward this sort of robotic behavior would be an act of dark sorcery and dominance and therefore opposed to the evolution of the individual and not something that the Shining Ones would do. The genius of their projected inspirations, and they are truly geniuses compared to us, is that the individual receiving the inspiration is inclined to think this is their own brilliant thought and embraces it readily.

As we stated earlier, the idea that is so often projected in the current media that psychic ability overwhelms the individual and is thus, as so often stated in these dramas, both a blessing and a curse, is not a problem the Shining Ones encounter. For them, psychic power is a blessing, although a blessing much on the same order as being able to speak, which those who are not mute tend to take for granted. Individuals who are overwhelmed by psychic impressions against their will and have no control over their ability are at the novice stages of developing this power.

The Shining Ones being strong individuals and secure in their unique nature have no difficulty sorting out what constitutes their thoughts and what comes from the outside of them, nor do they have any difficulty tuning out thoughts or impressions to which they have no need to listen. This filtering activity is not much different than most teenagers tuning out their parents, or any of us tuning out noise. For most of us, however, this can still be an effort when there is so much going on, while for the Shining Ones this is more easily accomplished, mostly because they have far more practice in doing so. We, too, can develop this power in the same way they did, which is to say using meditation, concentration and focus to let passing thoughts and extraneous noises evaporate before our consciousness.

The sort of traumatized activity that often accompanies psychic insight in movies is mostly dramatization. If a psychic endures that when they have a vision, then we can see how their power would seem a curse to hir and suggest regular and prolonged meditation as an antidote. The goal is to have psychic perceptions become as easy to experience and manifest as taking a shower.

As we've pointed out, this psychic power is only possible in it's more potent form because the Shining Ones are utterly secure in their own being, and at the same time, empathetic and compassionate toward others. It is this security of their individual ego that allows them to receive visions, or messages, without feeling like they are being invaded, as is the case with psychics and mediums that feel intruded upon by outside forces that in some cases temporarily take over their consciousness. The Shining Ones are never taken over by outside powers. They are never possessed. Nor do they possess others in the fashion it is done in Voudoun. However, in exceptional cases the Shining One can ride along with a willing carrier who retains their own consciousness even while being guided and inspired by an invoked Shining One. But primarily it is their empathy and compassion that allows the Shining Ones to see into the minds and hearts of others.

Most people see the world from their own point of view and no other. They cannot put themselves in another's shoes and thus have a very limited understanding of life and the world. But the Shining Ones, being extremely compassionate beings, have therefore a much wider view of life and see the Universe from a much broader perspective. The more we develop true compassion and empathy the greater will be our understanding of life and the more potent will our psychic powers be.

For most of us this compassionate understanding extends our

psychic ability to, as well as having a basic healing effect on, those that are currently around us. As we reach out to more and more people, we begin to get a glimpse into the evolution of whole ethnic groups and races. For the Shining Ones this power includes the power to look into previous chains of lifetimes, seeing the individual in their higher state, that is to say their true s'elf that survives and continues from one lifetime to another, and the potentialities of this course of manifestation, which is to say where they are likely to proceed in further lifetimes. This is also true concerning groups as well as individuals. Remember we are chained by our magic, which is to say our karma, to each other and we rise and fall for the most part together.

Which is why this is such a critical time for us all. More and more elves and others are pouring into the material world and assuming human bodies in an attempt to move the human race to a more satisfying future. The hope of these incarnating elves is to save billions upon billions of souls from having to be born as cockroaches in a world devastated by nuclear catastrophe or so far reduced in population by war, famine, disease and lack of essential resources that billions are forced back on the lower orders of evolutionary being. Our agents, the various elven and other proponents of sustainability, renewability, permaculture and a more intelligent use of resources, as well as a more compassionate way of dealing with each other, are, however, mostly ignored or derided, laughed at and scorned by the dark sorcerers of domination and the demons of destruction, but we still have hope. We have confidence in the magic we have created and faith in the essential goodness, if somewhat naïve nature, of humankind.

If the worse does come, then certainly many painful things will come for so many. Some of us, perhaps most, will go on to other dimensions, other globes to continue our evolution there. That is, in point of fact, how we came to the Earth/Elfin and got involved with man in the first place. Some of us, however, have become so karmically attached to man, through love and compassion and perhaps at times our own folly, that they will descend into the termite life and continue their work there if need be. However, being elves and thus ever a bit weird and different to most, we will no doubt be harassed or killed over and over again, lifetime after lifetime by our fellow ants, termites, cockroaches or whatever. Love, ain't it grand?

But we have every hope of a better future, and certainly will, for the most part, incarnate into the highest form available on this sphere. It is possible that after a few bumps, bruises and terrific potholes that humanity will set itself aright, more or less, and our evolutionary scheme will continue. Adaptability, after all, is a highlight of the Elven Way, or as we occasionally call it the Merry Way; and when all is said and done we will be on our Merry Way again.

And don't despair, beloved kindred, as you know this is not the first time humanity has violence-d and greed-ed itself into the toilet. There was Mu and there was Atlantis and here we are again and they don't seem like they've learned much from before, but they have really. Evolution is seldom fast and when it is, it tends to be catastrophic; so play the long game and know that in the vast scheme of things it will all work out as it is intended.

All this isn't, as it may seem, about the material survival of humanity, which is only an illusion anyway, but about the development of character, spirit and consciousness. The material seeming world is only a means to that end. It is about developing the personality into a radiant light of Elven magic that has the integrity and power to maintain its'elf in whatever dimensions it may find its'elf. And though we ever seek to improve our knowledge and our intellect, it is our wisdom and consciousness that is so much more important. It is more about soul-to-soul connection than mind-to-mind agreement. Thus one does not have to be a great thinker, intellect, or highly educated person to be a true example of Faerie light and power.

Spiritual insight is not so much about comprehending religious doctrines, dogmas or even magical formulas but about having a compassionate and deep understanding and empathy for one's others; thus seeing to the heart of reality and beyond the appearance and illusion of everyday life and the glamor/illusion of the world.

Magical power isn't about creating phenomena in the world, although one may indeed be able to do so, but about having the power to connect in a potent and influential way with other souls. One does not need, nor do elves often pursue, worldly positions of authority to do this; and we elves are never impressed by those who have such authority but lack the development of character that truly makes it powerful.

Thus the Shining Ones manifest among us in myriad ways. They may be rich or poor in worldly terms, have high social standing or be outcasts; they may appear beautiful or disguise their beauty in the glamor of ordinariness. They could be famous but more often are unknown to all but a few special ones. But what does distinguish them is a power of character and personality, an inner peace that is unmoved by the dramas of the world while being compassionate toward those poor souls who have bought into or fallen prey to such dark magics. There is almost always a sense of mystery about them that makes others wonder and marvel, for they are Faerie manifest, and that is ever a thing most wondrous and marvelous.

They expect and encourage us to ever be ours'elves, in fact, to continually deepen and develop our unique s'elfhood and our individual free spirit. At the same time in order to receive their guidance we must humble ours'elves enough to be open to it and allow ours'elves to be guided. Ever the way is one of balance, weaving this way and that, mixing that thing with this, spiraling round the Great Faerie Circle of the Dance of Divine Life, as we rise through the dimensions and planes of manifestation, becoming ever more that which we were always destined to be, which is our own true s'elves, Now and Forever More.

Thus we shall continue to tread the Elven Path and be on our Merry Way wishing you blessings many, love true, magic divine and a fervent hope that we will meet at the Great Gathering of the Elven Tribes Among the Stars.

> *It is most often better to have life be a bit of a drag than to have life dragging you.*
> —*Old elven Saying*

> "IN THE LONG RUN IT DOES NOT MATTER HOW YOU GET THERE AS LONG AS YOU DO GET THERE, AND YET IF YOU DON'T CHOOSE THE RIGHT WAY FOR YOU, YOU WILL GET LOST AGAIN AND AGAIN. THIS IS A PARADOX OF THE ELVEN WAY BUT ONE WITH WHICH ELVES BECOME INCREASINGLY COMFORTABLE AND IN DOING SO FIND THE WAY EVER MORE EASILY."
> —THE SILVER ELVES

The Elven Way

Ascending through dimensions
Closer we shall be
To all that we desire
In magical Faerie
And all there is that we must do
Is become the elves we seek
For it is we for whom we search
At the mountain's peak
The wisdom we do hunger for
Is our very own
Found in our own nature
As the wise have ever known
And Elfin that does call to us
Is found in our own heart
For where else would the magic be
That gave us each our start?
And yet as we become
Who we are meant be
We find that we are changing
Into all the light we see
In the ocean of the stars
In the sea of stellar light
We emerge as elvish brilliance
Awakened in the night

ABOUT THE AUTHORS

The Silver Elves are a family of elves who have been living and sharing the Elven Way since 1975. They are the authors of *The Book of Elven Runes: A Passage Into Faerie*; *The Magical Elven Love Letters, volume 1, 2, and 3*; *An Elfin Book of Spirits: Evoking the Beneficent Powers of Faerie*; *Caressed by an Elfin Breeze: The Poems of Zardoa Silverstar*; *Eldafaryn: True Tales of Magic from the Lives of the Silver Elves*; *Arvyndase (Silverspeech): A Short Course in the Magical Language of the Silver Elves*; *The Elven Book of Dreams: A Magical Oracle of Faerie*; *The Book of Elven Magick: The Philosophy and Enchantments of the Seelie Elves, Volume 1 & 2*; *What An Elf Would Do: A Magical Guide to the Manners and Etiquette of the Faerie Folk*; *The Elven Tree of Life Eternal: A Magical Quest for One's True S'Elf*; *Magic Talks: On Being a Correspondence Between the Silver Elves and the Elf Queen's Daughters*; *Sorcerers' Dialogues: A Further Correspondence Between the Silver Elves and the Founders of the Elf Queen's Daughters*; *Discourses on High Sorcery: More Correspondence Between the Silver Elves and the Founders of the Elf Queen's Daughters*; and *Ruminations on Necromancy: Continuing Correspondence Between the Silver Elves and the Founders of the Elf Queen's Daughter*.

The Silver Elves have had various articles published in *Circle Network News Magazine* and have given out over 5,000 elven names to interested individuals in the Arvyndase language, with each elf name having a unique meaning specifically for that person. They are also mentioned numerous times in *Not In Kansas Anymore* by Christine Wicker (Harper San Francisco, 2005), and *A Field Guide to Otherkin* by Lupa

(Megalithica Books, 2007). An interview with the Silver Elves is also included in Emily Carding's recent book *Faery Craft*.

The Silver Elves understand the world as a magical or miraculous phenomena, and that all beings, by pursuing their own true path, will become whomever they truly desire to be. You are welcome to visit their website at http://silverelves@live.com and join them on Facebook with name as the "Michael J. Love (Silver Elves)."

> "GREAT WEALTH SHOULD NOT IMPOVERISH OTHERS, BUT ENRICH THEM; OTHERWISE IT WILL IN TIME ITSELF BECOME GREATLY IMPOVERISHED."
> —THE SILVER ELVES

> "WATER RUNS IF YOU TRY TO GRASP IT, BUT POURS ON TO AN OPEN HAND."
> —OLD ELVEN SAYING

> "THROUGH THE FOREST SLIP SILENTLY; AMONG MEN, DO THE SAME."
> —THE SILVER ELVES

> "FROM THE SAME CLAY, WE ARE ALL MADE UNIQUE."
> —THE SILVER ELVES

> "A CIVILIZATION CAN BE JUDGED BY THE AMOUNT OF PUBLIC RESTROOMS THEY MAKE AVAILABLE."
> —THE SILVER ELVES

> "WHEN WE SAY THE ELVEN WAY, WE DO NOT MEAN ONE PATH THAT EACH AND ALL MUST TREAD WITHOUT EXCEPTION SAVE THAT EACH FINDS HIR OWN CREATIVE EXPRESSION IN HARMONY WITH LIFE AND CREATES THUS HIR OWN TRUE ELVEN WAY."
> —THE SILVER ELVES

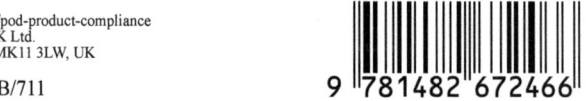